RUSSIA'S UKRAINE

NATO's Catastrophe

R. A. Romero

Rome Publications
Company

Printed in the United States of America.

For more information, or to book an event, contact: Info@romepublications.com www.romepublications.com

raromero@romepublications.com

https://romepublications.com/published-books/

Book design by Rome Publications

Cover design by Rome Publications

ISBN—Digital: 979-8-218-20051-0

ISBN - Paperback: 979-8-218-20052-7

ISBN - Hardcover: 979-8-218-20045-9

First Edition: August, 2023

Table of Contents

INTRODUCTION

We dread war because of its impact on history and how it changes us as a people, to say nothing of the lives that are lost. Homes and the fond memories we have of them are demolished—never to be seen again. War in the modern era is justified by a mask of nobility. The goal is to protect the greater good, while the actions of a few elitists start wars in order to continue with their historical legacy of pillaging and laying to waste, once great States, including Egypt, Syria, Iraq, Afghanistan, to name a few in recent history.

The Methods these countries use to justify their insurgency usually follow the same chronology and use the same deceptive propaganda which begins with the phrase: "Protecting Freedom and Democracy." Russia has a different perspective on the US intensions for Ukraine: "Encourage Ukraine to bomb ethnic Russians in order to force Russia to protect its people from genocide."

Some may claim that there is no good justification for war, but I maintain that the only real justifications, for war is one that prevents evil from becoming more powerful, in its quest for genocide. The Nazis, during World War II tried to cleanse Europe of the Jews and Pols, using murder by medical experimentation, starvation, and outright mass extermination. If not for the efforts of Russia, and later the United States, Hitler and the Third Reich would certainly have succeeded.

Now ethnic cleansing is more common than one might think. We are witnessing the irony of Israeli IDF driving the Palestinians from the west bank and other parts of the Old Testament borders of Israel, in the form of building high priced homes for Jewish settlers. In some cases, we see soldiers marching through neighboring territories, harassing and in some cases killing unarmed civilians in those territories. We see bull-dozers driving through Jenin tearing up the streets. This escalation of hostilities can only cease to exist when peace becomes the priority. I love the people of Israel, as I do people from Russia, China, Europe, the US, and those who strive for peace all over the world.

Another genocide, or population control, as one might call it, is the ethnic cleansing of a population by forcing people to leave their country in the form of refugees and allowing for mass immigration into its Western culture. Another would be the forcing children to adopt and embrace an ideology, sometimes by law, to make impressionable kids think it's ok not to have a normal relationship where they can procreate and have a family of their own—"Genocide by Propaganda" pushes society to the brink, by destroying the fabric of society, not to mention a danger to its population.

In this book, we analyze another event of aledged ethnic cleansing in the form of Ukraine driving out the pro-Russian and Russian citizens from Eastern Ukraine. I will reveal what most people are unaware of, that for eight years from 2014, Kiev has killed approximately 14,000 to 20,000 of its own citizens in the Donbass region of Ukraine. The West, of course, was silent. They did nothing to stop what Kiev was doing to its people.

We will see how the Russian Special military operation was forced to act because of the West's unwillingness to negotiate peace, and by providing more resources to the genocidal efforts of Ukraine since 2015.

This is a book of history that is derived from many sources, most verifiable, some not. No one can completely research the complete truth about something on the internet, but by showing a verifyable pattern of behavior, we can get closer to the truth. Events found in news articles and press conferences, by the very people involved, tell the whole story. You have heard the mainstream media's biased version of the war and taking every opportunity to deamonize Russia for its actions, so in a sort of balance, I will be telling more of the other side of the story that you probably haven't heard. This information slipped through the cracks of the mainstream narrative and paints the true picture of events taking place surrounding Russia's Special military operation. Events that reveal how dishonest our US government and our media really are.

It was very difficult finding un-biased references for this book, as Western media will show you atrocities, claiming Russia is to blame, only by the word of Kiev, but refuse to show any of the atrocities carried out by Ukraine. They burry reports from the CICE, the Red Cross, and others reporting on Ukraine's war crimes. They don't just report events but create articles analyzing those events with a slanted view of them, or rather, opion peaces disguised as news. Sadly, half the world is duped on the NATO/Urkaine narrative, and it is not necessarily the whole truth. That's why I was so compelled to write this book.

This war is just as ugly as any other—the devastation of which NATO is ultimately responsible for. This is not a book written to provoke hate, but rather to reveal the whole story not necessarily reported in Western media.

CHAPTER ONE

HISTORICAL REFERENCE CHANGES THE NARRATIVE

When Russia began its "Special Military Operation," the populous of America was 55% in support of Ukraine. However, as time passed and people began to research the truth about the history of Ukraine and the US State Department's involvement in Ukraine's political affairs, support shifted against Ukraine to 38%.[1] Just two years prior to the war, Western media outlets reported a plague of corruption and Naziism permeating Ukraine, now suddenly they are global heroes.

---

[1] Andrew Daniller, Andy Cerda
(27 August 2022)
https://www.pewresearch.org/short-reads/2022/09/22/as-war-in-ukraine-continues-americans-concerns-about-it-have-lessened/

THE 2 + 4 TALKS

On October 3rd, 1990, When Eastern and Western Germany were united once again, an agreement was made between the European countries of Great Britain, France, the two Germanies, and the Soviet Union. This was called the "2 + 4 talks." They addressed the security ramifications of Europe and Russia of a once again unified Germany. Those agreements were not legally binding; however, it was an agreement that Russia would take to heart addressing its border security concerns.

The talks reflected the desire of all parties involved to reduce tensions and promote stability in Europe at the time. However, it's important to note that any agreements or commitments made between countries, whether legally binding or not, should be respected if they remain in force. [2] The principle of "pacta sunt servanda," which is Latin for "Agreements must be kept," [3] is a principle that agreements must be respected by the parties that have entered into them, applies to both legally binding and non-legally binding agreements, which was the case for the agreements of the 2 + 4 talks. However, if the conditions upon which the agreement was

---

[2] Wikipedia Treaty
https://en.wikipedia.org/wiki/Treaty

[3] Wikipedia Pacta sunt servanda
https://en.wikipedia.org/wiki/Pacta_sunt_servanda

made changed significantly and can no longer be fulfilled, the agreement may be considered null and void. [4]

In any case, the integrity of any agreement depends on the willingness of the parties involved to abide by the terms of the agreement and to engage in good faith efforts to resolve any disputes that may arise. One of those agreements was that NATO would not expand East toward the border of Russia. [5]

The Soviet Union collapsed on December 31st, 1991.[6] Soon after, several Soviet States became their own independent republics, and NATO decided not to honor the security concerns of the new Russian Federation. The good faith to resolve the

---

[4] Swain, W. (2015). Classical contract law and its limits. In *The Law of Contract 1670–1870* (Cambridge Studies in English Legal History, pp. 201-230). Cambridge: Cambridge University Press. doi:10.1017/CBO9781139629324.009

[5] Wikipedia
Treaty on the Final Settlement with Respect to Germany
https://en.wikipedia.org/wiki/Treaty_on_the_Final_Settlement_wit
h_Respect_to_Germany
Note: Jürgen Chrobog, the Western German representative, stated that "during the 2+4 negotiations we made it clear that we [Germany] would not expand NATO beyond the Elbe. We cannot therefore offer Poland and the others NATO membership. NATO would conveniently leave that out of the agreement and later claim he was mistaken about what was agreed upon.

[6] Michael D M Timetoast timelines
https://www.timetoast.com/timelines/history-timeline-b25129b7-f9bc-4468-8980-227b3cdcbb5d

security concerns and obligation for Russia were never realized, under the 2 + 4 talks, NATO would claim the stipulation of expansion was never agreed upon.

Instead, NATO took advantage of the Power Vacuum that ensued and Incorporated the Czech Republic, Hungary, and Poland, in 1999; Bulgaria, Estonia, Latvia, Lithuania, Romania, Slovakia, and Slovenia in 2004; Albania and Croatia in 2009; Montenegro in 2017; and North Macedonia in 2020. [7]

NATO, led by the US has the distinct method of operation, (MO) of adopting Eastern European countries into NATO then planting missiles in those countries, moving closer and closer to Russia.[8] When the US interfered in Ukraine politics in 2014, President Putin began taking over Ukrainian territory to assure the West would not be allowed to adopt Ukraine into NATO, and thereby arming Ukraine with missiles along the Russian border.

Vladimir Putin, who was a Lieutenant in the Russian K.G.B. at the time of the collapse of the Soviet Union, would later, in his Presidency, continue to demand NATO respect the security concerns of Russia's borders.

---

[7] NATO (03 June 2022) A SHORT HISTORY OF NATO
https://www.nato.int/cps/en/natohq/declassified_139339.htm

[8] Wikipedia NATO missile defense system
https://en.wikipedia.org/wiki/NATO_missile_defense_system

US involvement in Ukrainian politics became apparent in 2004, with the Orange Revolution.

THE ORANGE REVOLUTION

In order to understand Russia's "Special Military Operation," we must begin with a brief history of Ukraine—dating back to the "Orange Revolution" of November 2004. Viktor Yushchenko and Viktor Yanukovych both won the Presidential election having two-fifths of the vote.

The following month there was a runoff vote that proclaimed Yanukovych the winner. Yushchenko's

Figure 1:Viktor Yushchenko was the principal leader of the Orange Revolution in 2004-- Courtesy Wikipedia

supporters declared that Yanukovych won by fraud and staged mass protests that came to be known as the Orange Revolution.

[9] Yushchenko was the principal leader of the Orange Revolution, along with Yulia Tymoshenko and others, which the West funded. [10]

Tymoshenko was a Ukrainian politician who became the first female Vice Prime Minister from 1999 to 2001, and ran for President in 2010, coming in second.[11] At the same time, the neo-NAZI movement infiltrated the Ukrainian government with Andriy Parubiy.[12] Parubiy was the Secretary of the National Security and Defence Council of Ukraine and the founder of the 1991 far-right "Social National

Figure 2: Yulia Tymoshenko, Ukrainian Politician, Presidential Candidate - 2010--Courtesy Wikipedia

---

[9] Britanica (19 February 2023)
Viktor Yushchenko https://www.britannica.com/biography/Viktor-Yushchenko

[10] Ian Traynor (25 November 2004)
US campaign behind the turmoil in Kiev
https://www.theguardian.com/world/2004/nov/26/ukraine.usa

[11] Wikipedia Yulia Tymoshenko
https://en.wikipedia.org/wiki/Yulia_Tymoshenko

[12] Wikipedia Andriy Parubiy
https://en.wikipedia.org/wiki/Andriy_Parubiy

Party of Ukraine"[13] with Oleh Tyhnybok, who both were followers of the Stepan Bandera movement.

Figure 3: Andriy Parubiy, founder of the farright Social-National Party of Ukrain--Courtesy Wikimedia Commons

Stepan Bandera was a political figure and mass murderer of Jews and Poles in WWII, who was a nationalist leader who fought Polish and Soviet rule in the 1930s and 1940s but is seen in Russia and eastern Ukraine as a Nazi collaborator.[14] Likewise, the Social National Party of Ukraine also had ties and overtones to the Neo-Nazi movement. Parubiy had a long history of politics in Ukraine until his resignation on August 29th, 2019. The Western media also knew Parubiy as the "Kommandant" of the Euromaidan movement, which occurred in 2013.

---

[13] Lev Golinkin (22 February 2019) Neo-Nazis and the Far Right Are On the March in Ukraine https://www.thenation.com/article/politics/neo-nazis-far-right-ukraine/

[14] Wikipedia Stepan Bandera
https://en.wikipedia.org/wiki/Stepan_Bandera

Two Candidates for the Presidential Election that year were Viktor Yushchenko, who represented the "Ukrainian Nationalists" party, which included many political parties,

including far-right groups. Viktor Yanukovych represented the "Party of Regions."[15] Yanukovych wanted deeper economic and political ties with Russia, while Yushchenko wanted to bring Ukraine into a closer Democratic-Socialist and economic relationship with the European Union.

Figure 4: Viktor Yanukovych, President of Ukraine 2010-2014--Courtesy Wikipedia

The incumbent government was accused of rigging the elections in Yanukovych's favor, so millions began protesting the election in Kiev. In Early 2005, Ukraine held another election, and this time Yushchenko won. The government was plagued with corruption, even awarding

[15] Wikipedia Party of Regions
https://en.wikipedia.org/wiki/Party_of_Regions

Ukraine as "The Most Corrupt Nation in Europe."[16] After five years of corruption and scandals, the voters aligned with the "Party of Regions" and elected Viktor Yanukovych again.

THE EUROMAIDEN REVOLUTION

In 2013, Ukrainian President Viktor Yanukovych failed to enter into trade agreements with the EU, which was backed by a large part of the population, the EU, and the United States. He stated that the accompanying IMF loan would return control of Ukraine's natural resources to the EU.[17] He also asserted that this would increase the cost of living for the average Ukrainian.

---

[16] Oliver Bullough (6 February 2015) Welcome to the most corrupt nation in Europe https://www.theguardian.com/news/2015/feb/04/welcome-to-the-most-corrupt-nation-in-europe-ukraine

[17] Luke Baker (5 March 2014) EU offers Ukraine $15 billion, but help hinges on IMF deal https://www.reuters.com/article/us-eu-ukraine-support-idUSBREA240V020140305

The people rose in opposition to Yanukovych, led by Andriy Parubiy,[18] once again and backed by the National Endowment for Democracy (NED)—A known front organization for the United States Central Intelligence Agency (CIA).[19] The protests began peacefully but grew increasingly violent, with citizens throwing Molotov cocktails and snipers shooting into the crowd. This would be known as the "Maiden Massacre,"[20] which prompted armed combatants to take over the government and the Civil War in the Donbass.

Figure 5: Ukrainian Euromaidan Revolution of 2014--Courtesy Wikipedia

---

[18] Rook Schrader, Jack Snyder, Graham Troy, David Newsham (10 November 2022) https://storymaps.arcgis.com/stories/2d29f5a174394b1e9866dd9d36b80213

[19] Kristin Christman (30 May 2022) The National Endowment for "Democracy": A Second CIA https://countercurrents.org/2022/05/the-national-endowment-for-democracy-a-second-cia/

[20] Bohdan Nahaylo (18 February 2020) Unsolved Maidan massacre casts shadow over Ukraine https://www.atlanticcouncil.org/blogs/ukrainealert/unsolved-maidan-massacre-casts-shadow-over-ukraine/

The newly formed government accepted the offer from the EU along with fifteen billion. However, the transaction increased natural gas prices to fifty percent higher than what Ukrainians

Figure 6: McCain with Oleh Tygnibok, leader of the Svoboda NAZI party--Courtesy maidantranslations.com

paid during Yanukovych's Presidency. [21]

Media outlets in the West claimed that the protests were peaceful the entire time and called it "The Flowering of Democracy." Utilizing the Neo-Nazi Svoboda Party, the US organized a coup that would topple the duly elected President of Ukraine, Viktor Fedorovych Yanukovych, on February 28th, 2014. The NED bussed people from outside the city and trained journalists to use television and social media to manipulate the events in their favor. This was further exacerbated by US

---

[21] BBC (26 March 2014) Ukraine agrees to 50% gas price hike amid IMF talks https://www.bbc.com/news/business-26758788

Senator John McCain, who supported the protest. Senator McCain, the then-ranking Republican on the Senate Armed Services Committee, went to Ukraine to show solidarity with the movement. McCain went on stage in Maidan Square, where he met with Oleh Tyagnibok, the leader of the Svoboda Nazi party.

Figure 7: US Undersecretary of State Victoria Nuland--Courtesy sadefenza.blogspot.com

US Assistant Secretary of State Victoria Nuland was caught in a leaked phone conversation conspiring to replace key personnel in Ukraine's new government. She was recorded saying:

"I think Yats [Arseniy Yatsenyuk] is the guy."

and discussing how to "glue this thing."[22] Nuland mentioned Svoboda's Tyahnybok as one of the leaders they were working with. A few weeks after the audio leaked, Yatsenyuk became the next prime minister of Ukraine. The conversation revealed that the Obama administration, and the US Ambassador to Ukraine,

were complicit in planning the coup against Yanukovych.

Until then, Russian President Vladimir Putin had enjoyed a sizable buffer zone of Allied states separating Russia from the threat of NATO countries.

President Yanukovych was pro-Russian, and a close ally of President Vladimir Putin. Yanukovych had no other recourse than to flee to Russia, where Vladimir Putin gave him asylum. Oleksandr Turchynov became the interim President and assumed power after the Ukrainian Revolution. His tenure lasted one hundred fifteen days during the time Vladimir

Figure 8: Russian President Vladimir Putin--Courtesy Wikimedia Commons

---

[22] BBC News (7 February 2014) Ukraine crisis: Transcript of leaked Nuland-Pyatt call https://www.bbc.com/news/world-europe-26079957

Putin invaded Ukraine and shortly after, the people voted to annex Crimea into Russia. [23]

Figure 9: Petro Poroshenko President of Ukraine, 2014 - 2019--Courtesy Wikimedia Commons

The candidates who were presented to replace him in the early elections in June 2014 were Yulia Tymoshenko and Petro Poroshenko. Poroshenko won the Presidency, receiving 54.7% of the votes cast, winning the election.

The founders, Oleh Tyahnybok and Andriy Parubiy of the Neo-Nazi Svoboda Party, would land leading roles in the newly formed Ukrainian government. Dmytro Yarosh led the "Right Sector"[24] delegation in Parliament and was appointed Parubiy's Deputy Secretary of RNBOU. Dmytro Yarosh also called himself a follower of Stepan Bandera.

---

[23] Wikipedia Timeline of the annexation of Crimea by the Russian Federation https://en.wikipedia.org/wiki/Timeline_of_the_annexation_of_Crimea_by_the_Russian_Federation

[24] BBC News (28 April 2014) Profile: Ukraine's ultra-nationalist Right Sector https://www.bbc.com/news/world-europe-27173857

Ukraine's Cabinet included members of two of the largest Neo-Nazi parties, the UNA-UNSO and the Svoboda, along with right-leaning elements. Their integration into the new regime placed them in charge of the Justice System, National Security, Armed Forces, and Police.

Oleh Makhnitsky of the Svoboda party was appointed Prosecutor General of Ukraine. Many other Right and Neo-Nazi affiliated members were appointed to key positions controlling the most critical aspects of the Ukrainian government. In addition, those still in government from the "Party of Regions" were soon expunged in targeted witch-hunts of the Lustration campaign.

We will find out later that NATO preferred the right-leaning groups to be in control of Ukraine because of their disdain for Pro-Russian groups and Russia herself. As a result, the US put into place a puppet government that they would later use as a proxy war against Russia, with the goal of toppling Putin's administration.[25]

---

[25] Anthony Zurcher (27 March 2022) Why Biden's off-script remarks about Putin are so dangerous https://www.bbc.com/news/world-us-canada-60895392

THE ANNEXATION OF CRIMEA

The day before the ousting of President Viktor Yanukovych by the newly installed NATO puppet government of Ukraine, approximately ninety heavily armed, professional pro-Russian gunmen seized the Parliament building and Council of Ministers building in Crimea on February 27th. President Putin denied the allegation that these armed forces were representatives of the Russian Military until much later.

Russia sent RF troops to the border of Crimea for military exercises. The Military presence was also to show intimidation to Ukraine, while troops in unmarked uniforms and militias stood watch, allowing the citizens of Crimea to organize their referendum. The citizens of Crimea voted nearly one hundred percent to be annexed back to Russia, and February 27th was reserved as a holiday to celebrate the seizure of Crimea by paramilitary forces.

Figure 10: Sergey Aksyonov Prime Minister of Crimea 2014 to present--Courtesy Wikimedia Commons

On March 1st, 2014, Sergey Aksyonov was appointed Prime Minister of Crimea. The first order of business was to appeal to Vladimir Putin, calling for Russia to "provide assistance in ensuring peace and tranquility on the territory" of Crimea. Afterward Thirteen Russian aircraft landed at the airport of Gvardeyskoye with two thousand paramilitary personnel in blue camouflage uniforms, suspected of being Russian Special Forces. This group took over the annexation of Crimea. Aksyonov was a member of the Russian Unity Party, the Russian Community of Crimea, and a member of the public organization "Civil Asset of Crimea." The West portrays Aksyonov as a career criminal with ties to the Russian Mafia, but Aksyonov denied the allegations. Aksyonov is a former member of the Russian paramilitary group, "Wagner Group." When Crimea was annexed, Aksyonov put together a para-military group of 300 men, Led by a former Wagner commander Konstantin Pikalov, from Africa. He called the paramilitary unit "Convoy" and used it to protect and calm the chaos in Crimea.[26]

President Putin explained: "The corruption in Ukraine corroded Ukrainian statehood, ultranationalists took advantage of this in 2014 with the support of the West."

The Russian Parliament backed Vladimir Putin's request to send soldiers to Crimea. Almost immediately, Crimea became part of the Russian Economy, with banks and other financial institutions and currency.

By a municipal law act, the Russian Federation annexed Crimea on March 21st, 2014. [27]

The United Nations saw this as an illegitimate action on behalf of Russia, which was expected by President Putin. Still, all

---

[26] Digital Forensic Research Lab (March 31, 2023) Russian War Report: A new private military company emerges in Crimea https://www.atlanticcouncil.org/blogs/new-atlanticist/russian-war-report-a-new-private-military-company-emerges-in-crimea/

[27] CBS News/ AP (16 March 2014) Crimeans vote overwhelmingly to secede from Ukraine, join Russia https://www.cbsnews.com/news/crimeans-vote-overwhelmingly-to-secede-from-ukraine-join-russia/

the actions of the Russian Federation were justified under international law and executed in a meticulous fashion.[28]

The UN supported Kosovo's referendum to be independent of Serbia, which now considers itself an independent state under the United Nations. The UN even participated by having NATO members launch a seventy-seven-day air campaign against Serbia in 1999, which killed many civilians. The UN also approved Slovenia's referendum to be independent of Croatia on December 23rd, 1990.

The UN didn't support the Donbass in its independence because they didn't want to side with the Russian Federation, which stands independent from the "Globalist Agenda" of a one-world government, led by the United States. Russia stands isolated as the one true Christian Nation left on the. The US "New World Order" was threatened by President Putin, and now he plans on creating his own "New World Order" with China.[29]

[28] UN (2014) The Yearbook of the United Nations 2014 Part 1: Chapter 5, Page 505-510 https://www.un.org/en/yearbook/2014/525

[29] Brendan Cole (21 July 2022) Putin Warns West Current World Order Is Over and New Era Is Coming https://www.newsweek.com/russia-putin-moscow-west-economics-world-order-1726686

THE DONBASS REFERENDUM

After the Maiden Massacre and the Annexation of Crimea in March 2014, The Donbass Descended into civil unrest. Anti-government separatists in Luhansk and Donetsk demanded independence from Ukraine's Fascist regime.

On May 11th, 2022, approximately one to two thousand anti-government protesters began occupying the Donetsk and Luhansk Security Services (SBU) buildings in an attempt to hold a referendum on April 7th, 2014. Separatists held the referendum to become a sovereign independent republic.

Dispite Kiev's Anti-Terrorist Operation" crackdown, targeting referendum organizers, which killed two civilians the day of the referendum, the turnout was still close to seventy-five percent, therefore, the commissions determined that the turnout was high enough to declare the referendum valid.

Kiev did not agree with the results because the voting process was claimed not to meet democratic standards. The referendum proved successful, however, with Donetsk receiving just over eighty-nine percent in favor of independence from Ukraine. Lugansk received over ninety-six percent. The people knew the consequences of their referendum, in that there would not be peace in the Donbass until Russia annexed them into the Motherland, as they did Crimea.

Kiev said the lack of polling places was unacceptable, and the turnout of the results was said to be exaggerated, with almost half of its citizens being locked down by the military. The UN claims, now, in 2022, that the voting was not regarded as legal under international law because armed soldiers brought polling boxes door to door. [30] Nevertheless, the people voted and dropped their private ballots in the secure ballot boxes, as with any free election, and a sovereignty of resolution was adopted. Donetsk and Luhansk became the "Donetsk People's Republic, (DPR) and Luhansk became the Luhansk People's Republic, (LPR), adopted on May 12th, 2014.

They had hoped by holding this referendum that they would be reunified with Russia, with the hope Putin would come to their aid to protect them from Kiev, but that wouldn't happen for eight more years. [31] Moscow publicly requested the referendum be postponed but supported its legitimacy.[32] Until

---

[30] UN News (27 September 2022) So-called referenda in Russian-controlled Ukraine 'cannot be regarded as legal': UN political affairs chief
https://news.un.org/en/story/2022/09/1128161

[31] Shaun Walker, Oksana Grytsenko (12 May 2014) Ukraine crisis: Donetsk region asks to join Russia
https://www.theguardian.com/world/2014/may/12/ukraine-crisis-donetsk-region-asks-join-russia

[32] Reuters Staff (7 May 2014) Putin urges Ukraine separatists to postpone referendum
https://www.reuters.com/article/us-ukraine-crisis-putin-referendum-idUSBREA460K420140507

that time, Kiev would continue to execute its "Anti-Terrorist Operation". [33]

Ukraine began bombing the Donbass region in 2014 to drive the Pro-Russian citizens out of the coal and oil-rich region and take back Luhansk and Donetsk from Russian influence, and to force armed protesters and unmarked soldiers, reported to be Russian, from the region. The result was bombing and killing soldiers and civilians in the LPR and DPR.

Moscow recognized the referendum's legitimacy and respected the people's choice in Donetsk and Lugansk and asked the EU to do the same. Moscow also requested that Kiev maintain a dialog with the DPR and LPR.

---

[33] Alec Luhn (15 April 2014) Ukrainian troops begin military operation to 'destroy foreign invader'
https://www.theguardian.com/world/2014/apr/15/ukrainian-troops-anti-terrorist-operation-kiev

GENOCIDE IN THE DONBASS

From 2014 to the Special military operation in February 2022, over 14,000 citizens of the Ukrainian Donbass region had been killed by the Kiev regime, intentionally and

Figure 11: Avenue of Angels memorial, Donbass--Courtesy Wikimedia Commons

unintentionally, including 101 children, with over 200 injured.[34] The "Avenue of Angels

---

[34] Diana Magnay, CNN (31 March 2016) Ukraine: Donetsk Citizens Crippled By War https://www.youtube.com/watch?v=1fsMqYqHnN0

CHAPTER TWO

HOW NATO PROVOKED
THE RUSSIAN INVASION

NATO and EU leaders proclaimed that Russia invaded Ukraine unprovoked. This, of course, was not true. NATO and Russia had provoked each other for many years—long before the Orange Revolution. With every passing year, NATO adopted more and more former Russian states into the organization, and American troops and missiles moved closer and closer to Russia, citing "Security in the region," but security from who?

THE US TRAINS UKRAINE FOR WAR AGAINST RUSSIA

NATO and the US failed to consider into their calculations that President Putin would retaliate against NATO's 2014 coup in Ukraine by invading Crimea. Likewise, due to Moscow's reprisal, the US sent three hundred paratroopers from the 173rd Airborne Brigade to begin training and arming the Ukrainian Ministry National Guard Units—the Neo-NAZI Azov battalion.[35] [36] [37]

These training exercises were approximately thirty miles away from the Polish border. Two thousand began training exercises in April. In addition, the US issued $19 million from the "Global Security Contingency Fund" to support Ukraine. [38]

---

[35] Sgt. A.M. LaVey (17 April 2015) 173rd Airborne Brigade arrives in Ukraine for Fearless Guardian
https://www.army.mil/article/146549/173rd_Airborne_Brigade_arrives_in_Ukraine_for_Fearless_Guardian/

[36] Aljazeera (1 March 2022) Profile: Who are Ukraine's far-right Azov regiment?
https://www.aljazeera.com/news/2022/3/1/who-are-the-azov-regiment

[37] Ben Watson (5 October 2017) In Ukraine, the US Trains an Army in the West to Fight in the East
https://www.defenseone.com/threats/2017/10/ukraine-us-trains-army-west-fight-east/141577/

[38] Bureau of Political-Military Affairs' Office of Congressional and Public Affairs (16 February 2023)
https://www.state.gov/the-global-security-contingency-fund/

The US has been conducting training with the Ukrainian military—teaching them how to organize their own training centers. In response, Moscow increased its support for rebels in the Donbass region.

The United Nations demanded that Russia sign the "United Nations Arms Trade Treaty," which would limit Moscow's support to anti-Ukrainian rebels in the Donbass region. Moscow refused. Mikhail Ulyanov, a representative of the RF Foreign Ministry's Non-Proliferation and Arms Control Department, criticized the agreement for being a "Too weak treaty."

"We don't have a negative attitude to this treaty, but we don't see the point of joining it..." [39]

The US was also providing weapons and training to Ukraine, specifically to use against the LPR and DPR at the time. Moscow has been providing support to the Rebels in Eastern Ukraine but did not provide the annexation they were hoping for. According to the defenseone.com website, Capt. Kayla Christopher of the US Army National Guard said,

"Our overall goal is to help the Ukrainian military become NATO-interoperable."

---

[39] Agence France-Presse (17 May 2015) Russia Will Not Sign 'Weak' Arms Trade Treaty https://www.defensenews.com/land/2015/05/17/russia-will-not-sign-weak-arms-trade-treaty/

Christopher also included that they wanted the Ukrainian military to have an opportunity to work with different countries—not just the US, but all their Slavic neighbors and all the other Western European countries.

US TRAINS UKRAINE IN THE TAKING BACK OF CRIMEA

Figure 12: Operation Rapid Trident, July 2015-- Courtesy Wikimedia Commons

"Operation Rapid Trident" began under the name "Peace Shield" from 1998 to 2002. It is a US European Command joint Training exercise conducted annually to enhance interoperability between European UN and NATO forces. The purpose of this joint training exercise was for the preservation of peace, cooperation, trust, and security in Eastern Europe.[40]

---

[40] Ben Watson (5 October 2017) In Ukraine, the US Trains an Army in the West to Fight in the East https://www.defenseone.com/threats/2017/10/ukraine-us-trains-army-west-fight-east/141577/

The operation included 15 countries with personnel varying between 1,300 to 2000 in any given year. Approximately two hundred US Soldiers participate in the exercise every year. In 2014, Ukrainian Defense Minister Valery Heletey said Some of the NATO states were helping Ukraine soldiers fight separatists in the Donbass region by arming them with weapons.[41] It was NATO's policy that it would not arm non-member states, but its members are allowed to arm Ukraine individually.

The United States had committed more than $1.3 billion in foreign assistance from 2014 to 2016. The US also provided Ukraine with $2 billion in loan guarantees, in 2017 US Congress approved an increase the budget to $3.42 billion for the "European Reassurance Initiative" (ERI).

This initiative, according to the Center for Strategic & International Studies, (CSIS), is to show US support in the Baltic region and invest in Presence; Training and Exercises; Infrastructure; Prepositioned equipment; and building partner capacity. It was used to add additional F-15s to NATO's Baltic Air Policing mission and to improve bases in Europe. The State Department also contributed funding to increase security

---

[41] BBC (14 September 2014) Nato members 'start arms deliveries to Ukraine' https://www.bbc.com/news/world-europe-29198497

assistance to non-NATO partners, including Georgia, Ukraine, and Moldova. [42]

The US Department of Defense claims from 2014 to February 28, 2023, the US has contributed $32.4 billion in security assistance to Ukraine over the course of eight years.[43] The Kiel Institute of Germany, however, reported that between Jan. 24, 2022, and Feb. 24, 2023, one year and one month, the US contributed more than $78.64 billion to Ukraine in Military asets, Humanitarian and Financial aid. [44] More than twice claimed by the DoD, and in just over one year.

During "Operation Allied Sky" in 2019, Which was an escalating show of force by NATO—Flying a number of fighter and bomber aircraft over thirty nations, two Russian Su-27s intercepted a US B-52 over the Black Sea, coming within 100 feet of the nose of the aircraft.[45] Jeff Harrigian of the USAF in Europe

---

[42] Mark F. Cancian (9 Febrary 2016) The European Reassurance Initiative https://www.csis.org/analysis/european-reassurance-initiative

[43] Jim Garamone (28 February 2023) NCOs Key to Ukrainian Military Successes Against Russia https://www.defense.gov/News/News-Stories/Article/Article/3313982/ncos-key-to-ukrainian-military-successes-against-russia/

[44] IFW Kiel Institute
Ukraine Support Tracker
https://www.ifw-kiel.de/topics/war-against-ukraine/ukraine-support-tracker/?cookieLevel=not-set

[45] Kyle Mizokami (1 September 2020) Not Cool: Watch a Russian Fighter Dangerously Buzz a U.S. B-52 Bomber

commented that these actions increased the potential for mid-air collisions and were unnecessary. Another B-52 was also intercepted by Russia over the Baltic Sea the following Friday.

In early September 2020, US B-52s conducted a training exercise with Ukrainian aircraft near the Russian territory of Crimea. Three B-52s flew a number of sorties near Crimea from the Royal Air Force (RAF) base in Fairford, UK. Though Crimea is still recognized by Ukraine as its territory, it has been completely annexed from Ukraine. Therefore, the Crimean penninsula is, by all geo-political and strategic considerations, Russian territory.

During this operation, Justin Bronk of the Royal United Services Institute (RUSI) commented,

"It was certainly an unusually open piece of military signaling by the US to the Russians and fits into a broader pattern of escalating posturing by both sides in recent months."[46]

---

https://www.popularmechanics.com/military/aviation/a33852860/russian-su-27-fighter-intercepts-american-b-52-bomber/

[46] Harry Lye (7 September 2020) US B-52s train with Ukrainian aircraft near Crimea https://www.airforce-technology.com/news/us-b-52s-train-with-ukrainian-aircraft-near-crimea/

RUSSIA AND BELARUS JOINT TRAINING EXERCISES

On November 29th, 2021, it was reported that Belarus announced Operation "Allied Resolve"—a military exercise to be conducted with Russian forces near the border of Ukraine. Lithuania said the Atlantic alliance needed to reposition toward Belarus, because of its increasing integration with Russia. Belarus accused the NATO military alliance of building up offensive capability near its borders. Defense Minister Viktor Khrenin said,

"We see troop formation around our state borders... We can only be concerned by the militarization of our neighboring countries, which is why we are forced to plan measures in response."

Alexander Lukashenko, the President of Belarus, said,

"Minsk would not sit idly on the sidelines if the simmering conflict in eastern Ukraine erupted or a war broke out with the West as Russia's borders." [47]

Belarusian Democratic Presidential candidate, Svetlana Tikhanovskaya, demanded the immediate withdrawal of Russian troops from the territory of Belarus. Representatives of the headquarters will seek to ensure that this issue is submitted

---

[47] Maxim Rodionov, Tom Balmforth, Gareth Jones (29 November 2021) Belarus announces military drills with Russia near Ukraine border https://www.reuters.com/world/europe/belarus-announces-military-drills-with-russia-near-ukraine-border-2021-11-29/

to the UN Security Council and called on the EU for new sanctions "that hit the regime, not the people."[48]

The following year, during Operation "Union Resolve 2022", Belarus and Russia set up three training and combat centers for the armed forces of Belarus and Russia. In addition, Russia sends Su-35 fighter jets to Belarus as part of an inspection of the reaction forces of the Union State. This was the launch of joint air-defense training and combat exercises. [49]

The operation also worked to "suppress and repel external aggression in the course of conducting a defensive operation, as well as countering terrorism and protecting the interests of the Union State."[50]

The United States condemned the joint training next to Ukraine's border as an "atmosphere of escalation with a gun to Ukraine's head." [51] As a result, on January 27th, 2022, the

---

[48] Idfo Vock (17 November 2021) Exclusive: Svetlana Tikhanovskaya calls for tougher EU sanctions on Belarus https://www.newstatesman.com/world/europe/2021/11/svetlana-tikhanovskaya-calls-for-tougher-eu-sanctions-on-belarus

[49] Military Drills (26 January 2022) First Russian Su-35S fighter jet arrives in Belarus for joint drills https://tass.com/defense/1393449

[50] Reuters (18 January 2022) Russia, Belarus to rehearse repelling external attack in joint drills https://www.reuters.com/world/europe/belarus-says-joint-drills-with-russia-run-feb-10-20-2022-01-18/

[51] Jennifer Hansler, Jeremy Herb, Kylie Atwood, Natasha Betrand, Rob Picheta, CNN (10 January 2022) US says no breakthrough in 'frank and forthright' talks with Russia over Ukraine border crisis

Pentagon announced military units had been placed on high alert for a possible Eastern Europe deployment. Those units included elements from:

- 18TH AIRBORNE CORPS AT FORT BRAGG & FORT, CAMPBELL, KY

- 82ND AIRBORNE DIVISION AT FORT BRAGG,

- 4TH INFANTRY AT FORT CARSON, CO, AND - 101ST AIRBORNE AT FORT CAMPBELL[52]

The White House announced it would approve plans for US troops to help Americans leave Ukraine if the Russian Federation invade. General Director of the Russian International Affairs Council, Andrey Kortunov:

"Should military operations begin, they will begin not because of the West, but because Ukraine might yield to the temptation to ruin the Minsk agreements and start an escalation in the east."[53]

---

https://www.cnn.com/2022/01/10/politics/us-russia-ukraine-meetings-geneva-intl/index.html

[52] Meghann Myers, Joe Gould (27 January 2022) These units from across the Army and Air Force are on alert for Ukraine deployment https://www.militarytimes.com/news/pentagon-congress/2022/01/27/these-units-from-across-the-army-and-air-force-are-on-alert-for-ukraine-deployment/

[53] Ukraine Crisis (26 January 2022) Wish to ruin Minsk-2 may push Kiev into war with Russia — expert https://tass.com/world/1393563 https://www.themoscowtimes.com/2021/09/23/zapad-2021-what-we-learned-from-russias-massive-military-drills-a75127

On January 31st, 2022, Ukraine had pulled heavy weapons and equipment into the Donbass in an attempt to hide it from the Organization for Security and Cooperation in Europe, (OSCE) SMM monitors. This was done with the help of electronic warfare systems and included weapons from the West. [54] This was aledged by the head of the LPR, Leonid Pasechnik.

By all accounts Russia initiated a build-up of troops, more and more as rhetoric from the US escellated, however, Operation "Zapad-2021", as well as other joint exercises have been conducted in prior years without such concern. [55] Ukraine President Zelensky said on February 2nd, 2022, he does not see a more significant escalation around Ukraine than it had been for the last year. Zelensky said:

"In the West, they give the impression that tomorrow there will be a war in Ukraine, but this is not so."

In fact, the rhetoric from DC was so bad Zelensky was forced to call a press conference with foreign media regarding the

---

[54] Idrees Ali, Phil Stewart (3 March 2022) U.S. providing intelligence to Ukraine, officials say https://www.reuters.com/article/ukraine-crisis-usa-intelligence-idUSL2N2V62MD

[55] Michael Kofman (23 September 2021) Zapad 2021: What We Learned From Russia's Massive Military Drills

Russian threat and call with Biden the day before. [56] He proclaimed:

"I'm the President of Ukraine, and I'm based here, and I think I know the details better here."[57]

President Zelensky announced $2.7 billion dollars was given to Ukraine this year by NATO, and now he is requesting an additional four billion—'to start with', while simultaneously admitting there is no concerning Russian aggression at this time. Zelensky went so far as to make statements that he was upset with the Biden Administration for its warmongering rhetoric, which was harming the Ukrainian economy.[58]

On February 12th, 2022, the Russian Ministry of Defense reported that a US Navy Virginia-class submarine was detected in the waters near the contested Kuril Islands in Russian

---

[56] David Brennan, Tom O'Connor, Naveed Jamali (2 February 2022) U.S. Accused of Hyping Russia Invasion of Ukraine, Frustrating Kiev, Moscow https://www.newsweek.com/us-hype-russia-invasion-intel-angers-moscow-rift-ukraine-1675313

[57] Michael Collins, Tom Vanden Brook (28 January 2022) Russian attack on Ukraine would bring 'significant' casualties, Gen. Milley says: What we know https://www.usatoday.com/story/news/politics/2022/01/28/ukraine-russia-says-wont-start-war-tensions-neighbor-soar/9251890002/

[58] Jason Melanovski (13 February 2022) Zelensky again rejects US claims of imminent Russian invasion even as Kiev continues war preparations https://www.wsws.org/en/articles/2022/02/14/ukr—f14.html

territory. The Virginia-class submarine entered an area where the Russian Pacific Fleet was conducting its scheduled exercises.

The Udaloy-class destroyer, the Marshal Shaposhnikov, discovered the sub and transmitted a message to the crew of the submarine in Russian and English in the underwater communication mode:

"You are in the territorial waters of Russia. Come up immediately!"

The demand of the Russian side was ignored. In accordance with the guidelines for the protection of the state border of the Russian Federation in the underwater environment, the crew of the frigate of the Pacific Fleet "Marshal Shaposhnikov" used appropriate means then drove the submarine from the area.[59]

The US Navy would viemently deny the allegations. US Navy Capt. Kyle Raines, a spokesman for US Indo-Pacific Command:

"There is no truth to the Russian claims of our operations in their territorial waters," said, in a statement. "I will not comment on the precise location of our submarines, but we do fly, sail and operate safely in international waters."[60]

---

[59] Jim Dean, Gordon Duff (12 February 2022) Breaking/Critical: Russia Discovers American Nuclear Sub in 'Firing Position' Inside their Territorial Waters https://www.veteranstoday.com/2022/02/12/breaking-critical-russia-discovers-american-nuclear-sub-in-firing-position-inside-their-territorial-waters/

[60] Howard Alman, Galina Tishchenko, Jim Heintz, Aamer Madhani (12 February 2022) Navy disputes Russia's claims that it chased a US sub

With global tensions at an all time high, it seemed logical that the US submarine would be monitoring the exercises and inadvertently sailed into what Russia considered, its territory. The EU was determined to punish Putin but was divided on how. Germany was receiving thirty two percent of natural gas from Russia and does not want to implement too harsh sanctions on Moscow. [61]

Australia and others were prepared to supply Germany with natural gas if Russia restricts Germany's energy. But Germany did not want to risk an energy crisis and a possible economic collapse just because of an operational exercise, so their sanctions against Russia were a watered-down version of what NATO requested.

---

out of its waters https://www.navytimes.com/news/your-navy/2022/02/12/russians-claim-they-chased-us-sub-out-of-their-waters/

[61] Vera Eckert, Kate Abnett (24 February 2022) Factbox: How dependent is Germany on Russian gas? https://www.reuters.com/world/europe/how-much-does-germany-need-russian-gas-2022-01-20/

THE WHITE HOUSE PROPAGANDA

White House National Security Advisor Jake Sullivan gave a press briefing on February 11th, 2022, announcing that Russia was planning to invade Ukraine "essentially at any time."[62] Sullivan claimed the Russian-Belarusian exercises on the Ukrainian border with Belarus were proof of an Imminent Invasion.

Ukraine claimed to have observed the deployment of Russian National Guard troops. On February 4th, 2022, the NYT reported that Russian Troops were in their final stages of readiness, adding to the increased concerns for Ukraine. The Ukrainian military high command reported:

"While the Russian military is not yet capable of mounting a total invasion of Ukraine, portions of its army have reached full combat strength and appear to be in the final stages of readiness for military action should the Kremlin order It."[63]

The head of the international committee of the US Senate, Robert Menendez, prepared what he called the "mother of all

---

[62] Melissa Quinn (14 Feburary 2022) Sullivan says Russia could launch Ukraine invasion "essentially at any time"
https://www.cbsnews.com/news/russia-ukraine-invasion-any-time-jake-sullivan-face-the-nation/

[63] Michael Schwirtz (4 February 2022) Russian Troops in Final Stages of Readiness Add to Worries for Ukraine
https://www.nytimes.com/2022/02/04/world/europe/russian-troops-ukraine-crimean-peninsula.html

sanctions," [64] which includes measures against the country's leadership, the main sectors of the Russian economy, and public debt. Menendez told reporters that these sanctions were in the event of a Russian invasion.

The Russian Federation began releasing videos of Eastern Military District units loading equipment onto trains heading to Belarus. On February 10th, 2022, the Russian Navy's Northern Fleet's Landing Vessels entered the Black Sea via the Bosphorus Strait. [65] White House officials began announcing that a Russian invasion would occur on February 15th, 2022.

After February 15th came and left without an invasion, the White House announced Russia's invasion would now take place on the 16th. [66] What is important to note here, is that Biden claimed that there would be a "Russian disinformation campaign to create a false flag", "that Kiev was attacking the

---

[64] The Economist (5 February 2022) America prepares the "mother of all sanctions" against Russia https://www.economist.com/finance-and-economics/america-prepares-the-mother-of-all-sanctions-against-russia/21807487

[65] Tony Roper (10 February 2022) Russian Navy moves large landing ships to Black Sea as exercise deployments continue https://www.janes.com/defence-news/news-detail/russian-navy-moves-large-landing-ships-to-black-sea-as-exercise-deployments-continue

[66] Bhavya Sukheja (12 February 2022) US President Biden Tells Western Allies Russia May Attack Ukraine On February 16: Report https://www.republicworld.com/world-news/us-news/us-president-biden-tells-western-allies-russia-may-attack-ukraine-on-february-16-report-articleshow.html

Donbass," and that he would use this as a precursor to an invasion.

On February 18th, 2022, Ukraine announced they intend to move against the Pro Russian rebels in the east, resulting in such a serious escellation, Denis Pushilin, the Head of the DPR posted a video message calling for "a mass centralized departure of the population to the Russian Federation".[67]

News agencies tried to portray the video as misinformation because the meta data showed it was recorded two days earlier. But the only thing the time of the recording proves is that the urgency to evactuate was imminent, and the evacuation plans were ready two days before it was announced.

Soon after calls of the evacuation, a car bomb detonated in downtown Donetsk, belonging to Donetsk's head of security. The explosion failed do kill its intended target.[68]

---

[67] Gianluca Mezzofiore (19 February 2022) Separatist leaders pre-recorded their video appeals, metadata shows
https://www.cnn.com/europe/live-news/ukraine-russia-news-02-19-22-intl/h_ce9740910a589f378762a6c2c3664e53

[68] Kyle Anzalone (18 February 2022) Fighting Intensifies In East Ukraine, Donetsk Leader Orders Evacuation
https://news.antiwar.com/2022/02/18/fighting-intensifies-in-east-ukraine-donetsk-leader-orders-evacuation/

Russia announced that it would begin to supply the pro-Russian rebels in the Donbass with weapons and supplies and help with the evacuation efforts.

Ironically, Secretary of State Antony Blinken visited Ukraine the week of January 19th, 2022, afterwards Biden announced a $200 million defensive military aid package to Ukraine. Additionally, the US State Department and Defense Department also quietly contributed an additional $2.7 billion, due to a "souring fear of a Russian invasion."[69][70] Ukraine used that money to buy and acquire more weapons from the West and even asked for additional funding.[71]

Russian President Vladimir Putin responded NATO's fears of a Russian-NATO conflict by suggesting, the only possible reasons for a Russia-NATO war would only happen if Ukraine were to join NATO or Kiev tried to take back Crimea, dragging both Russia and the bloc into war.

---

[69] Associated Press (19 January 2022) The U.S. will provide $200 million in military aid to Ukraine amid crisis https://www.npr.org/2022/01/19/1074020018/the-u-s-will-provide-200-million-in-military-aid-to-ukraine-amid-crisis

[70] USNI News (9 February 2022) Report to Congress on U.S. Security Assistance to Ukraine https://news.usni.org/2022/02/10/report-to-congress-on-u-s-security-assistance-to-ukraine

[71] Reuters (25 January 2022) Factbox: Ukraine gets weapons from the West but says it needs more https://www.reuters.com/world/europe/ukraine-gets-weapons-west-says-it-needs-more-2022-01-25/

Political Adviser for the State Department, Ned Price, made similar allegations that Russia was planning on staging a false flag operation in the Donbass as a precursor to an invasion. The fact was, there had been continuous battles in the Donbass between Ukraine and the rebels for the last eight years, and the Minsk 1 and 2 agreements were the result, but never fully realized.

The US Press Corp. was so dissolutioned by hearing continuous unsubstantiated claimes of a Russian invasion by the White House, that a reporter confronted Ned Price's narrative with the following:

"It's an action that you say they [the Russians] have taken, but you have shown no evidence to confirm that. This is like crisis actors? Really? This is like Alex Jones territory you're getting into now."[72]

In an interview with Euronews, Hungarian Foreign Minister Szijjarto said that the country would not participate in sanctions against the Russian Federation. He noted:

"If you look at the sanctions themselves, it's a failure. They don't work out. They are unsuccessful," he continued, adding that *"trade between Germany and the Russian Federation has increased since the sanctions have been in place."*[73]

---

[72] Hannah Grossman (3 February 2022) AP reporter spars with State Department's Ned Price over allegation on Russia: 'This is Alex Jones territory' https://www.foxnews.com/media/ap-reporter-spars-with-state-department-spokesperson-over-us-claim-on-russia-this-is-alex-jones-territory

[73] Euronews (10 February 2022) Ukraine crisis: Hungary won't accept more NATO troops on its soil, says foreign minister Szijjártó

Szijjarto also called for doing everything possible to avoid a "new cold war" and conflict between Russia and the West.

The Organization for Security and Co-operation in Europe, (OSCE), is an organization of monitors from many independent states. They have been reporting on hostilities between the pro-Russian rebels in the Donbass and Ukrainian forces since 2014. The website describes their Special Monitoring Mission to Ukraine, (SMM), as follows:

"The SMM was an unarmed, civilian mission, operating on the ground 24/7 in Ukraine. Its main tasks are to observe and report."

The OSCE describes themselves as an impartial and objective manner on the security situation in Ukraine and to facilitate dialogue among all parties to the conflict."[74]

The following week, Ukrainian forces used weapons provided by the US and its NATO allies to increase the shelling on Donetsk and Luhansk, as reported by the OSCE.

The OSCE logged 553 explosions in Donetsk and 860 explosions reported in Luhansk, the weekend of February 19th, 2022. In total more than 1500 violations of the Minsk agreement

https://www.euronews.com/2022/02/09/ukraine-crisis-hungary-won-t-accept-more-nato-troops-on-its-soil-says-foreign-minister-szi

[74] OSCE (31 March 2022) OSCE Special Monitoring Mission to Ukraine (closed) https://www.osce.org/special-monitoring-mission-to-ukraine-closed

were violated.[75] The increase in fighting on the front lines prompted observers to proclaim the shelling in and around Donetsk is the most intense they have seen in years.[76]

At this time, the provication was so obvious, and the attacks so brutal, Russia had no choice but to prepare to send its forces to Ukraine. In a last-ditch effort for peace, Russian Prime Minister Sergei Lavrov asked President Putin to continue along the diplomatic path in its efforts to extract security guarantees from the West.[77]

Joe Biden continued to push his accusations about an unprovoked invasion by Russia many times during the week. His staff would also hold press conferences corroborating the accusations with other members of the Defense Department, the UN, and EU—all cooberating eachother based solely from Jake Sullivan's and Joe Biden's narrative.[78]

---

[75] Reuters (19 February 2022) OSCE reports surge in number of explosions in east Ukraine https://www.reuters.com/world/europe/osce-reports-surge-number-explosions-east-ukraine-2022-02-19/

[76] Jamie Dettmer (19 February 2022) Shelling, Mortar Fire Intensify in Ukraine's Donbas as War Clouds Gather https://www.voanews.com/a/shelling-mortar-fire-intensify-in-ukraine-s-donbas-as-war-clouds-gather-/6450218.html

[77] Reuters (14 February 2022) Russia's Lavrov urges Putin to allow more time for diplomacy amid Ukraine crisis https://www.reuters.com/world/europe/russias-lavrov-proposes-russia-continue-diplomatic-work-european-security-push-2022-02-14/

[78] Katie Bo Lillis, Jim Sciutto, Jeremy Herb, Matthew Change, Kylie Atwood (23 February 2022) US warns full-scale invasion of Ukraine

Ukrainian officials claimed that Russia had deployed an additional 10,000 troops to the region of the Crimean Peninsula. Those include infantry and airborne forces. More concerning to Ukrainian military assessment, Russia put their troops on the highest level of readiness.

It seems conclusive that Biden provoked the escellation and supposed "False Flag" event he warned about, by funding Ukrainian which allowed the AFU to increase hostilities against the pro-Russian forces in the Donbass.

THE WORLD REACTS

EU foreign policy chief Josep Borrell said that Europe was in its 'most dangerous' security moment since the Cold War.[79]

The US had discussions with the EU days ago about the possibility of Asian countries, including China, to deliver natural gas to Europe in the event of an escalation in Ukraine.[80]

---

could be imminent https://www.cnn.com/2022/02/23/europe/russian-troops-donbas-latvian-pm/index.html

[79] Aljazeera (7 February 2022) Europe faces 'most dangerous moment' over Russia-Ukraine tensions https://www.aljazeera.com/news/2022/2/7/europe-faces-most-dangerous-moment-amid-russia-ukraine-tensions

[80] Jennifer Jacobs, Annmarie Hordern (2 February 2022) Biden Scours Globe to Send Europe Gas If Russia Hits Ukraine

Sergey Naryshkin, the Head of the Foreign Intelligence Service of the Russian Federation, made the statement that Russia did not have aggressive plans toward Ukraine and that Russia's plans to attack Ukraine are war propaganda cooked up in the US State Department.[81]

On February 20th, 2022, on Face the Nation, Russian Ambassador to the United States, Anatoly Antonov said:

"There is no invasion, and there [are] no such plans."[82]

Even the North Korean Foreign Ministry called the US statements about Russia's invasion of Ukraine, "wild rumors." Ex-US Computer consultant and Naturalized Russian citizen Edward Snowden said on Twitter:

"There is nothing more grotesque than a media pushing for war."[83]

---

https://www.bloomberg.com/news/articles/2022-02-02/u-s-talks-to-china-japan-india-about-sending-gas-to-europe?leadSource=uverify%20wall

[81] Reuters (21 February 2022) Russian spy chief Naryshkin accuses U.S. of war propaganda https://www.reuters.com/world/europe/russian-spy-chief-naryshkin-accuses-us-war-propaganda-2022-02-21/

[82] Mellissa Quinn (20 February 2022) Russian ambassador insists Kremlin has "no such plans" for invading Ukraine despite troop build-up https://www.cbsnews.com/news/russia-ukraine-ambassador-anatoly-antonov-no-such-plans-invasion-face-the-nation/

[83] Jessica Corbett (11 February 2022) 'Nothing More Grotesque Than a Media Pushing for War,' Says Edward Snowden https://www.commondreams.org/news/2022/02/11/nothing-more-grotesque-media-pushing-war-says-edward-snowden

After a week of continuous sound bites of an eminent Russian invasion by the Media, it became clear that the White House wanted an invasion, even claiming that it was already occurring,[84] and that the goal of a Russian Invasion was "Regime Change" to remove Zelensky from power. This turned out to be false. Zelensky is still in power to the day of this publication. In fact, President Putin promised former Israeli prime minister Naftali Bennett, a year later, that he would not kill Zelensky.[85]

The campaign was expected to be two days of aerial bombardment and electronic warfare and then an invasion.

At this time, the OSCE was being rearranged and relocated outside of its ability to monitor the activities in the Donbass effectively, and possibly influenced negatively by their new relocations.

According to the organizers of the OSCE, "certain participating states" instructed their people, totalling twenty-one personnell, to leave the mission within the next few days but were told to continue to carry out its duties of monitoring Ukraines activities from their states. Organizers placed thirty

---

[84] Quint Forgey (22 February 2022) White House official: 'This is the beginning of an invasion'
https://www.politico.com/news/2022/02/22/white-house-beginning-invasion-russia-ukraine-00010589

[85] Tia Goldenberg, AP (4 February 2023) Former Israeli PM: Putin promised not to kill Zelenskyy
https://abcnews.go.com/International/wireStory/former-israeli-pm-putin-promised-kill-zelenskyy-96901897

others in "Ukrianian controlled territory," away from the hostilities, sighting concerns for its citizens.[86]

Russian foreign ministry spokeswoman Maria Zakharova said that the OSCE:

"informed the participating states of the decision by 'a number of countries' to relocate their national staff of the OSCE Special Monitoring Mission to Ukraine 'due to deteriorating security conditions.'"

Zakharova claimed that the move served to heighten tensions over Ukraine saying:

"These decisions cannot but cause our serious concern." and *"The mission is purposefully dragged into militaristic psychosis pumped by Washington and used as a tool for possible provocation."[87]*

Though it remains to be seen if the concerns of the RF over the OSCE's deployment were ever realized, considering the invasion took place ten days later.

US National Security Adviser then emphesised:

---

[86] Joseph Choi (13 February 2022) US staff at OSCE withdraw from rebel-held eastern Ukraine city: report
https://thehill.com/policy/international/594064-us-staff-at-osce-withdraw-from-rebel-held-eastern-ukraine-city-report/

[87] TASS News (13 February 2022) Zakharova: the OSCE mission in Ukraine is used as a tool for possible provocation
https://tass.ru/politika/13695233

" I do think the world should be prepared for Russia staging a pretext and then launching a potential military action"[88]

Secretary Blinken announced on Twitter:

"Kremlin recognition of the so-called Donetsk and Luhansk People's Republics as "independent" would signify Russia's wholesale rejection of the Minsk agreements, which remain the best means to resolve the conflict in the Donbass."[89]

Blinken however, failed to mention that Ukraine was in violation of the Minsk agreements by its increased attacks on Donetsk and Luhansk, according to the OSCE.

It was apparent, at this point, that the US was instigating the Russian invasion of Ukraine with the increased attacks on its pro-Russian citizens in the Donbass.[90]

The buildup of one hundred fifty thousand plus Russian troops was apparent, but still not as significant as one might expect. With "Operation Union Resolve" taking place, which

---

[88] Tim Hains (13 February 2022) National Security Advisor Jake Sullivan: The World Must Be Prepared for Russia To Stage A Pretext For War In Ukraine This Week https://www.realclearpolitics.com/video/2022/02/13/national_security_ad visor_jake_sullivan_the_world_must_be_prepared_for_russia_to_stage_ a_pretext_for_war_in_ukraine_this_week.html

[89] Secretary Antonyt Blinken @SecBlinken (16 February 2022)

[90] France24 (16 February 2022) US accuses Moscow of creating Ukraine invasion pretext with 'genocide' claims https://www.americanchronicles.news/the-us-ensures-that-more-than-40-of-russian-troops-on-the-border-with-ukraine-are-in-attack-position/

amassed thirty thousand troops,[91] and about sixteen thousand in Crimea,[92] leaves approximately seventy-five thousand, which was the amount of troops recorded along the Ukrainian Russian border since 2021, according to the Center for Strategic & International Studies, (CSIS).[93]

Heavy Military Aviation aircraft was relocated from inside Russian Aerospacial Forces in Siberia to Western Russia near the Ukrainian border.

President Zelensky played off the threat on February 19th, when Vice President Kamala Harris met with him at the Munich Security Conference. When Molly Nagle asked if Zelensky agreed with Biden that Putin had already decided to invade Ukraine, he replied in english:

"Nice to meet you."

---

[91] Paul Mcleary, Alexander Ward (19 February 2022) Russian military build-up continues, despite Moscow's promises of a drawdown https://www.politico.com/news/2022/02/19/russian-military-build-up-continues-despite-moscows-promises-of-a-drawdown-00010372

[92] Ron Synovitz (4 March 2014) Russian Forces In Crimea: Who Are They And Where Did They Come From? https://www.rferl.org/a/russian-forces-in-crimea—who-are-they-and-where-did-they-come-from/25285238.html

[93] Mykola Blelleskov (21 September 2021) The Russian and Ukrainian Spring 2021 War Scare https://www.csis.org/analysis/russian-and-ukrainian-spring-2021-war-scare

Minutes later, reporters asked again, and he did not respond.

An interesting article by the CATO Institute on December 14th, 2020, lays out the case that NATO might have provoked Russia to amass troops along it's borders due to historic military buildup of NATO troops in Poland, among other places.[94]

BRICS AND OTHER RUSSIAN ALLIANCES

Brazil

Brazil's President Jair Bolsonaro visited Vladimir Putin at the Kremlin on February 16th, 2022, "to discuss global affairs and streanthen Brazil and Russia's strategic partnership and cooperation in trade."[95] The US voiced its outrage over the meeting. Jen Psaki, the White House press secretary, announced that it was time to accuse Brazil of "attacking the Global Values"

---

[94] Ted Galen Carpenter (14 December 2020) Is NATO Provoking the Russian Military Build-up in Kaliningrad? https://www.cato.org/commentary/nato-provoking-russian-military-build-kaliningrad

[95] Gov.br (16 February 2022) President Jair Bolsonaro and President Vladimir Putin meet in Moscow https://www.gov.br/en/government-of-brazil/latest-news/2022/president-jair-bolsonaro-and-president-vladimir-putin-met-in-moscow

for expressing solidarity with Russia amidst the tensions on the Ukraine-Russia border. A US Reporter in the press corp. asked Psaki:

"President Bolsonaro of Brazil met with Putin this week in Moscow. He expressed solidarity with Russia. Does the President [Joe Biden] feel betrayed?"

Psaki Responded:

"I think Brazil may be on the other side, on the opposite side of where the majority of the global community stands."[96]

In response, the Ministry of Foreign Affairs of Brazil published the following statement:

"The Ministry of Foreign Affairs regrets the content of the White House spokesman's statement regarding the President of the Republic's statement on the occasion of his visit to Russia.

Brazil's positions on the situation in Ukraine are clear, and have been repeatedly transmitted to the authorities of friendly countries and expressed within the United Nations Security Council, (UNSC). The Ministry of Foreign Affairs does not consider it constructive or useful..."[97]

---

[96] Lisandra Paraguassu (18 February 2022) White House rebukes Brazil's Bolsonaro for 'solidarity' visit to Moscow https://www.reuters.com/world/americas/white-house-rebukes-brazils-bolsonaro-solidarity-visit-moscow-2022-02-18/

[97] Gov.br (19 Febraury 2022) Statements regarding Brazilian foreign policy https://archive.is/slOmb#selection-3377.0-3377.45

Venezuela

Venezuelan President Nicolás Maduro offered Russia the full support of Venezuela to confront NATO in the face of the crisis in Ukraine:

"We have reviewed the powerful military cooperation, and we have ratified the path of a powerful military cooperation between Russia and Venezuela for the defense of peace, of sovereignty, the defense of territorial integrity,"

"We are going to increase all the preparation, training and cooperation plans with a military power in the world such as Russia."[98]

India

India remained reluctant to take sides, but at the UNSC on February 17th, 2022, India called for immediate de-escalation through sustained diplomatic efforts and also for addressing legitimate security concerns of all countries. [This was to include Russia's security concerns.]

The Russian embassy in India tweeted with a thanks soon after, saying:

---

[98] AP (16 February 2022) Venezuela's leader pledges military cooperation with Russia https://news.yahoo.com/venezuela-russia-hold-discussions-west-185152195.html

"We welcome India's balanced, principled, and independent approach."[99]

China

Chinese leader Xi Jinping's made a four-day visit to Russia on March 21st, 2023, in which Xi and Putin showed the world the mutual cooperation of thier countries' ties and pledged to "deepen military mutual trust."

Putin remarked of military cooperation between China and Russia calling it:

"...one of the most important areas that strengthens the remarkably trusting, strategic nature of relations,"

Li told Putin that trust between the two countries' militaries has been "increasingly consolidated" and cooperation has yielded "fruitful results," according to Chinese state media.[100]

---

[99] Times of India (18 February 2022) India's big Ukraine problem: To go with US or Russia" https://timesofindia.indiatimes.com/india/indias-big-ukraine-problem-to-go-with-us-or-russia/articleshow/89666744.cms

[100] Simone McCarthy (April 17, 2023) US-sanctioned Chinese defense minister meets Putin in Moscow, hails military ties https://edition.cnn.com/2023/04/16/china/china-defense-minister-visit-russia-vladimir-putin-li-shangfu-intl-hnk/index.html

South Africa

In January 2023, supporters of the new regime of Burkina Faso took to the streets waving Russian flags.

They spoke highly of Russia's deployment of mercenaries in Libya, Mali, and the Central African Republic (CAR) to fight off Islamist insurgents, saying:

"The Russians got good results in other African countries."

President Putin has strengthened relations in Africa for many years. Putin and Egyptian President Abdel Fattah el-Sisi co-chaired the first Russia-Africa Summit, which assembled 43 African heads of state in Sochi. Russia also signed a $12.5 billion in deals with African countries.[101]

Now, more than nineteen countries want to join BRICS.

---

[101] Samuel Ramani (17 February 2022) Russia Has Big Plans for Africa https://www.foreignaffairs.com/articles/africa/2022-02-17/russia-has-big-plans-africa?check_logged_in=1

MERCENARIES AND AGENTS OF THE RUSSIAN FEDERATION

PMC Wagner, one of Russia's Mercenary groups, is considered a long arm military unit of Russia. In 2022, they consisted of fifty thousand troops stationed around the world and two hundred thousand reservists. Other Russian mercenaries include: RSB-Group, Antiterror, MAP, MSGroup, Centre R, ATK Group, SlavCorps, ENOT, and Cossacks. Seven of which would be called to participate in the invasion of Ukraine. Their success in retaking lost territories in Ukraine would capture the attention of US politicians, who later designate them a "Terrorist Organization."

Figure 13: PMC Wagner Group Logo—Courtesy PMC Wagner

Figure 14: Ramzan Kadyrov meeting with Presdient Putin June 2018--Courtesy Wikimedia Commons

The Chechnyan military would also play an enormous role in the Special Military Operation. Ramzan Kadyrov, Leader of the region of Chechnya would be tasked to coordinate the attack on Kiev.[102] Kadyrov is a Colonel General in the Russian military and was tasked to coordinate the offensive against Kiev.

Kadyrov, and his forces are fearcely comfortable in battle and had reported playing a significant role in capturing Ukrainian territory. They have also made videos which claimed their forces had rescued many Ukrainians that had been held as human shields by the Azov batallion.[103] [104]

Kadyrov made the statement and urged Ukrainians to:

"rise up against their own government" which he said was "made up of neo-Nazis."[105]

Western media would prodominently post articles about Chechens taking up arms against Russia and would ignore the success of the pro-Russian Chechens fighting forces executing its mission in Ukraine.

---

[103] Vic Children of the Light on Facebook (27 March 2022)
https://www.facebook.com/watch/?v=758562955119385

[104] Pro-Kadyrov Channel on Telegram (19 March 2022)
https://t.me/Kadyrovite/118

[105] Reuters (26 February 2022) Chechen leader, a Putin ally, says his forces deployed to Ukraine
https://www.reuters.com/world/europe/russias-chechen-leader-says-his-forces-deployed-ukraine-2022-02-26/

Ramzan Kadyrov himself, would become a celebrity, of sorts with his pro-Russian audience, where Kadyrov participated in two comedy skits where a President Zelensky look-alike was captured and brought to Kadyrov for execution,[106] another skit depicted Zelensky surrendering Ukraine. [107] It was a jab at Zelensky who made skits just like this as a comedian before he became President of Ukraine.

Kadyrov would also later be a target of critisizm of the West by suggesting on Telegram:

"In my personal opinion, more drastic measures should be taken, right up to the declaration of martial law in the border areas and the use of low-yield nuclear weapons." [108]

Kadyrov was also known for criticizing the Russian forces leadership describing Colonel-General Alexander Lapin, commander of the Russian forces fighting at Lyman, as a "mediocrity", and suggested that he should be demoted to private and stripped of his medals.

Russian Foreign Minister Sergei Lavrov's claimed that 'mercenaries' from Tirana, Pristina, and Sarajevo were heading

---

[106] Russian insider (11 July 2022)
https://www.youtube.com/watch?v=vGBP5Yb4juM

[107] Dare Da Don (4 July 2022)
https://www.youtube.com/watch?v=8HRQFofr8-o

[108] Reuters (1 October 2022) Kadyrov says Russia should use low-yield nuclear weapon https://www.reuters.com/world/europe/russia-says-its-troops-left-lyman-avoid-encirclement-2022-10-01/

to the front lines in Ukraine. There are Jihadists in Ukraine, but many of them are Tatars, and some are Chechens. Jihadists exist on both sides, but Chechens mainly side with the LPR and DPR, while Tatars side with Ukrainians. Balkan Muslims have not been seen as a prominent participator of the conflict.

Ankara supports Jihadist militants in Ukraine, but sources report that they're waiting for a war to transpire in Crimea. Turkey mainly uses Tatar networks and fighters from Syria in Ukraine. Many of these Tatars set up networks in Ukraine and joined Al Qaeda along with other Syrian rebel groups. Some analysts accuse Turkey of having plans to send additional Jihadists to link up with the Tatars in the event of war.

Why Turkey? Turkey considers Crimea its rightful territory. Many Tatars went to Syria to fight Russia after Crimea joined the Russian Federation. They want to kick the Russians out of Crimea and use their favor and influence gained to enable increased Turkish influence in Ukraine, particularly Crimea.

Tatars are part of the Turkish proxy war against Russia in Syria, and their mercenaries are believed to be participating in multiple proxy war conflicts elsewhere.

Belarus hasn't participated in the war in Ukraine, except to facilitate the invasion from its country, but has always advocated for peace.[109]

N A T O   F O R C E S

In response to Russia's heightened readiness in the region, the US sent troops to bolster NATO's eastern flank. Those numbers were as follows:

- One thousand troops are being moved from Germany to Romania;

- Two thousand troops from the US are being deployed to Poland and Germany;

- Eight thousand five hundred troops in the US have been placed on a heightened state of alert.

Overall, NATO forces totaled approximately fourty-thousand on the western border of Ukraine, with an estimated 300,000 on heightened alert.[110]

---

[109] Isabel Van Brugen (31 March 2023) Belarus Urges 'Truce' as Putin's Closest Ally Calls for War to End https://www.newsweek.com/belarus-lukashenko-ceasefire-truce-russia-ukraine-war-1791787

[110] Euronews (18 May 2022) NATO now has 40,000 soldiers on Europe's border with Russia https://www.euronews.com/my-

THE DONBASS AND RUSSIAN ALLIANCE

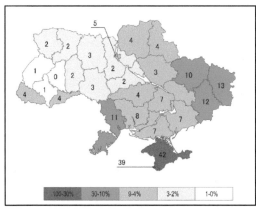

Figure 15: Russians who voted "No" on becoming Ukraine--Courtesy Wikimedia Commons

The Donbass has historically been a no-man's land for outlyers, People without a home. Culturally, it has been prodominently inhabited by ethnic Russians, Jews, and others. [111] Ukraine, itself has been the victim of many battles in the past and taken over by many countries. The Soviet Union adopted Ukraine in 1937 and has been Russia until the collapse of the Soviet Union in 1991.[112]

When Ukraine became an independent state, after the collapse of the Soviet Union, 96% of the people voted to become

europe/2022/05/18/nato-now-has-40-000-soldiers-on-europe-s-border-with-russia

[111] Ronald Suny (21 February 2022) A historian corrects misunderstandings about Ukrainian and Russian history https://theconversation.com/a-historian-corrects-misunderstandings-about-ukrainian-and-russian-history-177697

[112] Wikipedia 1991 Ukrainian Referendum https://en.wikipedia.org/wiki/1991_Ukrainian_independence_referendum

independent. The Donbass region, Crimea, and Odessa region voted 30% to 100% against leaving Russia.

After 1991, the Eastern region of Ukraine has historically voted for pro-Russian candidates. [113] The people in that region were particularly dissalusioned with the 2014 election which ousted their duly elected President. Afterwards, Donetsk and Luhansk wanted to be annexed to Russia, just as Crimea was.

Russian influence has always dominated eastern Ukraine, even after 1991. Russia state radio and television broadcasted pro Russian news and information in the Donbass region. Up until 2014, President Putin has had unrestricted influence in Ukraine as it does Belarus. After the 2014 coup, President Putin lost influence to NATO, and was going to make sure he still had some control over the region to keep a buffer zone between Russia and NATO.

---

[113] Wikimedia Commons Search Result: "Ukraine Voting" https://commons.wikimedia.org/w/index.php?search=ukraine+voting&titl e=Special:MediaSearch&go=Go&type=image

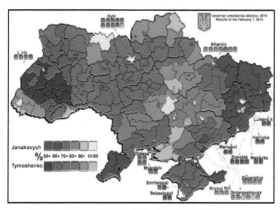

Figure 16: Voting in Ukraine, 2010--Courtesy Wikimedia Commons

Currently, with the increased shelling by the AFU in the Donbass region, the Kremlin has become more involved with the security and humanitarian concerns of the LPR and DPR. Moscow announced that the Russian Federation would launch an investigation into mass graves found in Donbass. This signaled to NATO that Russia was about to increase its alliance with the Donbass and would begin to intervene in the region. [114]

In response to the increased Shelling of the Donbass and the humanitarian crisis created as a result, Moscow announced that starting, February 18th, a mass centralized departure of the population to the Russian Federation has been organized. First, women, children, and the elderly are subject to evacuation. "We kindly ask you to listen and make the right decision. Temporary departure will save the life and health of you and your loved ones." It was announced:

---

[114] Reuters, Alexander Ermochenko (16 February 2022) Russia claims mass civilian graves found in Donbas
https://www.jpost.com/international/article-696703

"By agreement with the leadership of the Russian Federation, places for the reception and accommodation of our citizens are ready in the Rostov Region. The evacuees would be provided with everything necessary. All conditions had been created for a quick transition at checkpoints."[115]

Though Western media and the Biden Administration would report that there is no proof of an evacuation, the DPR showed videos of hundreds of citizens being loaded into doezens of busses and trains heading to Russia—Putin announcing they would receive accommodations and ten thousand rubles each.[116]

[115] Reuters (18 February 2022) Separatist leader in eastern Ukraine announces evacuation of residents
https://www.reuters.com/world/europe/separatist-leader-eastern-ukraine-announces-evacuation-residents-2022-02-18/

[116] Nikolai Trishin TASS News (18 February 2022) East Ukraine Separatist Regions to Evacuate Civilians to Russia
https://www.themoscowtimes.com/2022/02/18/east-ukraine-separatist-regions-to-evacuate-civilians-to-russia-a76452

CHAPTER THREE

PUTIN'S MOVE TO EVADE WAR, MARRED BY FRUSTRATION

History will always show that Vladimir Putin was the first one to step up with negotiations to overt a war between Russia and Ukraine in 2022. The Demands requested by the Kremlin are derived from decades of prior agreements that, to this day, have never been taken seriously by the US' and UK's NATO. Unfortunately, the US' refusal to compromise in any way frustrated the Russian negotiators, which responded unfavorably, causing the crisis to move to its inevitable conclusion, war.

RUSSIA DEMANDS SECURITY GUARANTEES

Putin has insisted that the territory of Ukraine is being used for threats against Russia.[117]

The Security Guarantees proposed by Russia were an attempt to deter war between NATO/Ukraine and Russia. The talks were discussed by Russia and the United States in a closed format in Geneva on January 10, 2022.[118] The Russian delegation was represented by the Ministry of Foreign Affairs and the Ministry of Defense. The US delegation was led by US Deputy Secretary of State Wendy Sherman.

Speaking to reporters, Sergey Ryabkov said:

"The United States needs to be prepared to make compromises. Russia has come here with a clear position, which contains a number of aspects that, in my view, are easy to understand and

---

[117] Sky News (22 February 2022) Putin: 'Ukrainian territory is used for threats against Russia' https://news.sky.com/video/putin-ukrainian-territory-is-used-for-threats-against-russia-12548695

[118] Emma Farge (10 January 2022) U.S. and Russia still far apart on Ukraine after Geneva talks https://www.reuters.com/world/europe/prospects-dim-us-russia-start-tense-talks-over-ukraine-crisis-2022-01-10/

are formulated so clearly, particularly at the top level, that it is impossible to deviate from our approaches." [119]

Almost all Western news outlets would fail to list President Putin's five general, and reasonable security guarantees. Boris Johnson would claim of the negotiations as:

"President Vladimir Putin is holding a gun to Ukraine's head in a bid to bully the West into redrawing the post-Cold War security map of Europe."

Putin had five general guarantees that were not that unreasonable, but the US would refuse to give up influence over any of Europe.

1. Putin wanted NATO to agree that Ukraine was not joining NATO, and that staging weapons on the border between Russia and Ukraine was a "red line" for Moscow. [120]

2. The Kremlin also demanded that Washington and its alliances would excluding Ukraine, Georgia or any other ex-Soviet nations of its NATO expansion.

3. NATO is to also agree not to station any troops in areas where they weren't present in 1997—before NATO moved to incorporate former Soviet bloc countries and ex-Soviet republics.

---

[119] TASS News (9 January 2022) US should be ready to make compromises at Geneva talks — senior Russian diplomat https://tass.com/politics/1385425

[120] Reuters (1 February 2022) Putin is holding a gun to Ukraine's head, UK's Johnson says https://www.reuters.com/world/uk/uks-johnson-russia-sanctions-will-kick-immediately-if-it-invades-ukraine-2022-02-01/

4. Moscow also suggest a freeze on patrols by Russian and U.S. naval ships and bombers near each other's territories.

5. To make efforts to reduce the risk of incidents involving Russia and NATO warships and aircraft, primarily in the Baltic and the Black Seas; a reduction of military drills; greater transparency, and other confidence-building measures. [121]

According to William Alberque, the Director of Strategy, Technology, and Arms Control at the International Institute for Strategic Studies, (IISS), the draft proposal drew heavily from the 2009 Russian proposal of the Agreement on Basic Principles Governing Relations among NATO-Russia Council Member States in Security Sphere. [122]

In order to better comprehend the spirit of Putin's Security Demands, I included a summary of the 2009 Proposal, referenced by William Alberque. This proposal references six other Accords and Agreements—all of which bring us to the closest possible understanding of what Russia's security demands likely entailed. The US response in the next chapter also references Article 1 of the draft:

---

[121] Andrew Roth (17 December 2021) Russia issues list of demands it says must be met to lower tensions in Europe https://www.theguardian.com/world/2021/dec/17/russia-issues-list-demands-tensions-europe-ukraine-nato

[122] Andrey A. Baklitskiy (14 January 2022) Putin's demand for security guarantees: Not new and not to be taken literally, but not to be ignored https://thebulletin.org/2022/01/putins-demand-for-security-guarantees-not-new-and-not-to-be-taken-literally-but-not-to-be-ignored/

The Charter of the United Nations (1970)

The Charter of the United Nations outlines the structure and purposes of the United Nations. It was adopted in 1945 by the United Nations Conference on International Organization and came into force on October 24, 1945. The Charter has been amended once by the Protocol of the Sixtieth Session of the General Assembly.

The Charter consists of a preamble and 111 articles, divided into 19 chapters. The articles set out the objectives, principles, and organisation of the United Nations, as well as its functions and powers. The Charter also establishes the Security Council, the General Assembly, the Economic and Social Council, the International Court of Justice, and the Secretariat.[123] [124]

The Helsinki Final Act of the Conference for Security and Cooperation in Europe (1975)

1975 Helsinki Final Act, also known as the Helsinki Accords, was a set of agreements adopted at the Conference on Security and Cooperation in Europe (CSCE) in 1975. The conference was held in Helsinki, Finland, and was attended by representatives

[123] UN Basic Facts: The Charter of the United Nations
https://www.un.int/news/basic-facts-charter-united-nations

[124] UN United Nations Charter (Full Text) https://www.un.org/en/about-us/un-charter/full-text

from thirty-four European countries, the United States, and Canada. [125]

The Helsinki Final Act included agreements on a wide range of issues, including human rights, economic cooperation, and security issues. It also established the basis for ongoing dialogue and cooperation among the participating countries on these issues. The Helsinki Accords was seen as an important step in improving relations between the Soviet Union and the West during the Cold War. [126]

NATO-Russia Founding Act, (1997)

The Founding Act on Mutual Relations, Cooperation, and Security between the North Atlantic Treaty Organization (NATO) and the Russian Federation, also known as the NATO-Russia Founding Act, is a 1997 agreement that established a framework for relations between NATO and Russia.

The agreement was signed in Paris on May 27, 1997. The act provided for regular consultations between the two sides and established a Permanent Joint Council, (PJC) to facilitate

---

[125] CSCE (1 August 1975) The Helsinki Final Act
https://www.csce.gov/international-impact/publications/helsinki-final-act

[126] OSCE (1 August 1975) Helsinki Final Act (Full Text)
https://www.csce.gov/sites/helsinkicommission.house.gov/files/Helsinki%20Final%20Act.pdf

cooperation on issues, including arms control, counter-terrorism, and crisis management.

It also set out a commitment by both sides to respect each other's sovereignty, territorial integrity, and independence and to refrain from the threat or use of force against each other. Additionally, the act committed both sides to respect the principles of the United Nations Charter and the principles of the Conference on Security and Cooperation in Europe (CSCE) and to work towards the creation of a stable, peaceful, and undivided Europe.

The Founding Act was seen as an important step towards improving relations between NATO and Russia and was seen as a way to build confidence and increase transparency between the two sides. [127] [128]

OSCE Code of Conduct, (1994)

The 1994 Code of Conduct on Political-Military Aspects of Security, also known as the OSCE Code of Conduct, is a set of guidelines and principles for the conduct of relations between states in the field of security. The Code of Conduct was adopted

---

[127] NATO (27 May 1997) Summary Founding Act on Mutual Relations, Cooperation and Security between NATO and the Russian Federation https://www.nato.int/cps/en/natohq/official_texts_25470.htm?selectedLo cale=en

[128] NATO (12 October 2009) Founting Act (Full Text) https://www.nato.int/cps/en/natohq/official_texts_25468.htm

by the Organization for Security and Cooperation in Europe (OSCE) at the Budapest Summit in 1994.

The Code of Conduct lays out a number of principles for the management of relations between states in the field of security, with the aim of promoting transparency and stability. These principles include commitments to respect the sovereignty, territorial integrity, and independence of all states, to refrain from the threat or use of force against other states, and to resolve disputes through peaceful means.

It also emphasizes the importance of dialogue and cooperation between states and encourages the adoption of measures to reduce the risk of armed conflicts. The Code of Conduct is non-binding, but it serves as a set of guidelines for the OSCE member states to follow, and it has been considered an important tool in maintaining security and stability in Europe.[129] [130]

The Rome Declaration "NATO-Russia Relations: A New Quality", (2002)

The Rome Declaration "NATO-Russia Relations: A New Quality" was adopted in 2002 at the NATO-Russia Summit held

[129] Ursula Froese (13 October 2010) The Code of Conduct on Politico-Military Aspects of Security: a sleeping revolution https://www.osce.org/fsc/104195

[130] OSCE (1994) Code of Conduct on Politico-Miulitary Aspects of Security (Full Text) https://www.osce.org/files/f/documents/5/7/41355.pdf

in Rome, Italy. It represents a new phase in the relationship between NATO and Russia and lays out a vision for a more cooperative and constructive relationship between the two sides.

The Declaration emphasizes the commitment of both sides to the principles of the United Nations Charter and the OSCE and to the resolution of disputes through peaceful means. It also commits both sides to work together to address common security challenges, such as terrorism, proliferation of weapons of mass destruction, and regional conflicts. Both the 1999 Charter on European Security and the Rome Declaration are important documents in promoting security and cooperation in Europe.[131]

The draft of the European Security Treaty, (2008)

On June 5, 2008, the President of Russia put forward an initiative to develop a new pan-European security treaty, the main idea of which is to create—in the context of military and political security in the Euro-Atlantic region—a common

---

[131] Cambridge University Press (18 May 2017) North Atlantic Treaty Organisation (NATO)-Russian Federation: Declaration by Heads of State and Government of NATO Member States and the Russian Federation (NATO-Russia Relations: A New Quality) https://www.cambridge.org/core/journals/international-legal-materials/article/abs/north-atlantic-treaty-organisation-natorussian-federation-declaration-by-heads-of-state-and-government-of-nato-member-states-and-the-russian-federation-natorussia-relations-a-new-quality/A3829AB8AE23CDDB5E9F19A7A2D2CCDB

undivided space in order to finally do away with the Cold War legacy.

In view of this, Dmitry Medvedev suggested formalizing in the international law the principle of indivisible security as a legal obligation pursuant to which no nation or international organization operating in the Euro-Atlantic region is entitled to strengthen its own security at the cost of other nations or organizations.

Based on the results of discussions that have taken place in the last year at various venues, Russia has prepared a draft European Security Treaty. The Russian President has sent this draft to the heads of relevant states and to chief executives of international organizations operating in the Euro-Atlantic region, such as NATO, the European Union, the CSTO, the CIS, and the OSCE. [132]

Dmitry Medvedev emphasized that Russia is open to any proposals on the subject matter of its initiative and counts on the positive response from its partners and the beginning of a substantial discussion on specific elements of the draft treaty. A partial clip of the text is given below:

---

[132] President of Russia (29 November 2009) The draft of the European Security Treaty http://en.kremlin.ru/events/president/news/6152

December 4, 2009, Agreement on Basic Principles Governing Relations Among NATO-Russia Council Member States in Security Sphere

The Member States of the NATO-Russia Council (NRC) - Parties to this Agreement (hereinafter referred to as the Parties), committed to promote friendly relations between States for the benefit of a lasting and comprehensive peace in the Euro-Atlantic region founded on the principles of democracy, market economy and the rule of law; recognizing that uniting efforts of all the Parties is indispensable to respond effectively to contemporary challenges and threats to security in a globalized and interdependent world; seeking to bring their relations to a new level through equal partnership, solidarity and mutual trust in the sphere of security; noting that security interests of each Party call to improve effectiveness of multilateral cooperation, enhance stability, predictability and transparency in the political and military sphere; reaffirming their commitment to the purposes and principles of the Charter of the United Nations; the 1975 Helsinki Final Act adopted at the Conference on Security and Cooperation in Europe; the 1997 Founding Act on Mutual Relations, Cooperation and Security between the North Atlantic Treaty Organization and the Russian Federation; the 1994 Code of Conduct on Political-Military Aspects of Security; the 1999 Charter on European Security and the Rome Declaration "NATO-Russia Relations: A New Quality" signed by the Heads of State and Government of NATO Member States and the Russian Federation in 2002. The Articles included:

Article 1: Illustrate the need for NATO to cease expansion;

Article 2: to facilitate a framework for which parties can peacefully settle disputes;

Article 3 & 4: Demands that NATO not station specific munitions, aircraft, troops permanently, but does provide for a forty-two day exercise where these munitions and personnel may be allowed;

Articles 5, 6, and 7 Discussion of arms-control measures, and ratification of the agreement.[133]

Article 8: To solve contemporary challenges and threats to security jointly. [134]

Russia has continued to put forth and was instrumental in the negotiations of, many such treaties and agreements which help to strengthen mutual cooperation with respect to territorial and regional security but have mostly fallen on deaf ears. The United States has an unwillingness to be bound by any such agreements proposed by Russia.

---

[133] Bits.de (4 December 2009) Agreement on Basic Principles Governing Relations Among NATO-Russia Council Member States in Security Sphere https://www.bits.de/NRANEU/US-Russia/NR-DraftTreaty2009ocr.pdf

[134] Memri (1 March 2022) Confidential NATO, U.S. Responses to Russian Demand For Security Guarantees, Known As 'Putin's Ultimatum,' Prior To Invasion Of Ukraine https://www.memri.org/reports/confidential-nato-us-responses-russian-demand-security-guarantees-known-putins-ultimatum#_ednref3

The United States demands other countries utilize the existing diplomatic instruments and structured framework for its negotiations, which are completely advantageous to the desired direction and control of the United States.

President Putin speaking about a possible invasion of Ukraine, at a news conference in Moscow December 23, 2021, said:

"This is not our (preferred) choice, we do not want this."[135]

The negotiations in Geneva continued for 7.5 hours. Sergei Ryabkov, the Deputy Foreign Minister of the Russian Federation announced:

"There is a basis for reaching an agreement with the United States and NATO on security guarantees, the search for a balance of interests is possible."[136]

In another statement Ryabkov expressed frustration saying:

"Attempts by the United States and NATO to blackmail and intimidate Russia are unacceptable, they will not give results!"[137]

---

[135] Reuters (23 December 2022) Putin says Russia doesn't want conflict but needs 'immediate' guarantees
https://www.reuters.com/world/europe/putin-we-dont-want-conflict-over-ukraine-2021-12-23/

[136] Intel Slava Z (10 January 2022) https://t.me/intelslava/16288

[137] Al Mayadeen (10 January 2022) US threats, blackmail will not work against Russia: deputy FM
https://english.almayadeen.net/news/politics/us-threats-blackmail-will-not-work-against-russia:-deputy-fm

Ryabkov said that Russia needs reinforced concrete guarantees that Ukraine and Georgia will never become members of NATO. The iron guarantees of Ukraine and Georgia's non-entry into NATO will be the entry of Ukraine and Georgia into the CSTO.

A frustrated Ryabkov insinuating NATO was attempting to blackmail and intimidate Russia, returned with an interesting response of blackmail and threats of his own:

"If our opponents on the other side - above all the United States but also other countries, its allies, so-called like-minded countries - if they refuse, and try and torpedo this, they will inevitably get a further worsening of their own security situation," [138]

NATO Secretary General, Jens Stoltenberg made the following statements on the meeting of the NATO—Russia Council:

"NATO's relationship with Ukraine is going to be decided by the 30 NATO allies and Ukraine, no one else,"

European Commission President Ursula von dr Leyen made the statement:

---

[138] Reuters (10 December 2021) Russia urges NATO to break promise to Ukraine as part of security package
https://www.reuters.com/world/europe/russia-demands-rescinding-nato-promise-ukraine-georgia-2021-12-10/

"Aggression needs to come with a price tag, which is why we will communicate these points ahead of time to Russia." [139]

Despite Russia's aggressive negotiations, I believe NATO could have been more creative, rather than stubborn, to come to some compromise that would have prevented the invasion.

---

[139] AlJazeera (10 December 2021) NATO chief rejects Russian demand to deny Ukraine entry https://www.aljazeera.com/news/2021/12/10/nato-refuses-to-backtrack-on-ukraine-georgia-membership-promise

CHAPTER FOUR

THE WEST REJECTS PUTIN'S SECURITY GUARANTEES

The argument of who violated prior Agreements first should not dictate the actions of NATO to address Russia's security concerns— especially now, but it had, and the US response was stubbornly ineffectual, and the result—war.

THE WEST RESPONDS TO PUTIN'S SECURITY GUARANTEES

The United States and Western allies put together a nine-page response regarding the talks in Geneva. Referenced were the following Treaties, Talks, and Agreements mentioned in the US response:

Minsk 1 and Minsk 2 agreements, (2014, 2015)

The Minsk Agreements are a set of agreements signed in the Belarusian capital of Minsk in 2015, aimed at resolving the ongoing conflict in eastern Ukraine between Ukrainian government forces and Russian-backed separatists. The first Minsk agreement, known as Minsk 1, was signed on September 5, 2014, and called for a ceasefire, the withdrawal of heavy weapons, the release of prisoners, and constitutional reform in Ukraine to give greater autonomy to separatist-held regions.[140] [141]

---

[140] Wikipedia (2014) Minsk agreements
https://en.wikipedia.org/wiki/Minsk_agreements

[141] OSCE (2014) FOLLOWING THE CONSULTATIONS OF THE TRILATERAL CONTACT GROUP ON JOINT STEPS AIMED AT IMPLEMENTING THE PEACE PLAN OF THE PRESIDENT OF UKRAINE P. POROSHENKO AND THE INITIATIVES OF THE PRESIDENT OF RUSSIA V. PUTIN (Russian Only)
https://www.osce.org/files/f/documents/a/a/123258.pdf

Minsk 2 was signed on February 12, 2015, building on the provisions of Minsk 1. The agreement includes 13 points, which among other things, calls for the immediate and full ceasefire, the withdrawal of heavy weapons, constitutional reform in Ukraine to give greater autonomy to separatist-held regions, the release of all hostages, and the return of control of the border to Ukraine.[142]

Both Minsk agreements have been widely seen as the framework for resolving the conflict in eastern Ukraine; however, the ceasefire has been violated repeatedly, and the agreements were never fully implemented.

The 1990 Charter of Paris for a New Europe, (1990)

The 1990 Charter of Paris for a New Europe, also known as the Paris Charter, was a political declaration signed by the leaders of thirty-four European and North American countries on November 21, 1990. The charter affirmed the commitment of signatories to democracy, the rule of law, and the protection of human rights and fundamental freedoms. It also recognized the right of all nations to self-determination and the inviolability of European borders. Additionally, the charter called for the strengthening of economic and political cooperation in Europe and the promotion of peace, stability, and security. The signing

---

[142] UN Digital Library (17 February 2015) Resolution 2202 (2015) / adopted by the Security Council at its 7384th meeting, on 17 February 2015 https://digitallibrary.un.org/record/787968

of the charter marked the end of the Cold War and the beginning of a new era of cooperation in Europe.[143] [144]

The Istanbul Charter for European Security, (1999)

The Istanbul Charter for European Security, also known as the Istanbul Summit Declaration, was a political declaration adopted by the heads of state and government of the Organization for Security and Cooperation in Europe, (OSCE) at the OSCE summit in Istanbul, Turkey in 1999. The charter reaffirmed the commitment of the participating states to the principles of the Helsinki Final Act and the Charter of Paris for a New Europe, including respect for human rights and fundamental freedoms, the rule of law, and the inviolability of borders. The charter also emphasized the importance of a comprehensive approach to security, which includes economic, humanitarian, and environmental factors, as well as military and political aspects. The Istanbul Charter for European Security also set out the OSCE's goals for the future, which include the

[143] OSCE (21 November 1990) CHARTER OF PARIS FOR A NEW EUROPE (Full Text) https://www.osce.org/files/f/documents/0/6/39516.pdf

[144] OSCE (21 November 1990) Paris Summit 1990 and the Charter of Paris for a New Europe (summary) https://www.osce.org/paris-summit-1990-and-charter-of-paris-for-a-new-europe

promotion of democracy, the protection of human rights, and the strengthening of regional stability and security.[145]

The Normandy Format, (2015)

The Normandy Format is a diplomatic group comprising of four countries: France, Germany, Russia, and Ukraine. The format was established to address the ongoing conflict in Eastern Ukraine and the annexation of Crimea by Russia. The leaders of these four countries have met several times in an effort to reach a peaceful resolution to the conflict and to address issues related to the implementation of the Minsk agreements, which were signed in 2015 to end the fighting in eastern Ukraine. The group takes its name from the location of the first meeting between the leaders of the four countries, which took place in Normandy, France in 2014.[146] [147]

The Trilateral Contract Group, (2014)

The Trilateral Contact Group on Ukraine (also known as the Trilateral Contact Group for the peaceful settlement of the

---

[145] OSCE (1999) Istanbul Summit (Charter for European Security)
https://www.osce.org/files/f/documents/4/2/17502.pdf

[146] Wikipedia (2014 – 2021) Normandy Format
https://en.wikipedia.org/wiki/Normandy_Format

[147] CSIS (9 February 2022) Understanding the Normandy Format and Its Relation to the Current Standoff with Russia
https://www.csis.org/analysis/understanding-normandy-format-and-its-relation-current-standoff-russia

situation in eastern Ukraine) is a group of representatives from Ukraine, the Russian Federation, and the Organization for Security and Co-operation in Europe. that was formed in May of 2014, as means to facilitate a diplomatic resolution to the war in the Donbass region of Ukraine. There are several subgroups.[148]

The Geneva International Discussions, (2008)

The Geneva International Discussions (GID) is a format for negotiations aimed at resolving the conflict in and around Georgia, which began with the 2008 Russia-Georgia war. The GID was established in 2008, following the war and brings together representatives of the European Union, the United Nations, and the Organization for Security and Cooperation in Europe (OSCE) as well as representatives from the Russian Federation, Georgia, the United States, and the breakaway regions of Abkhazia and South Ossetia. The main objective of the GID is to provide a platform for dialogue and to address security and humanitarian issues arising from the conflict, including the return of refugees and internally displaced persons, and the restoration of economic and other links. The GID is also aimed at preventing an escalation of the situation on

---

[148] OSCE Database (2014) News and press releases
https://www.osce.org/press-releases/trilateral%20contract%20group?filters=+ds_date:([2014-01-01T00:00:00Z%20TO%202015-01-01T00:00:00Z])&solrsort=score%20desc&rows=50&category=News

the ground and to contribute to stability and security in the region.[149]

5+2 Transnistria Settlement Talks, (1990)

The 5+2 format is a negotiation process involving representatives from the Transnistria, Moldova, Russia, Ukraine, and the OSCE (Organization for Security and Cooperation in Europe), as well as observers from the European Union and the United States. The format of the talks is also known as the "5+2 Transnistria Settlement Talks" or "5+2 Dialogue." The purpose of these talks is to resolve the long-standing conflict between Moldova and the breakaway region of Transnistria, which declared independence from Moldova in 1990 but has not been recognized by any UN member states. The talks focus on issues related to security, political, and economic issues, with the ultimate goal of finding a peaceful and lasting settlement to the conflict.[150]

---

[149] OSCE Database (2008) News and press releases
https://www.osce.org/press-
releases?filters=%20i18n_tus_en_field_keywords%3A%22Geneva%20I
nternational%20Discussions%22%20im_taxonomy_vid_1%3A%289%29
%20im_taxonomy_vid_3%3A%28116%29&solrsort=ds_date%20desc&r
ows=10

[150] US Mission to the OSCE (30 November 2017)
https://osce.usmission.gov/52-talks-transnistrian-settlement-process-2/

The Conventional Armed Forces in Europe (CFE) Treaty, (1990)

The Conventional Armed Forces in Europe (CFE) Treaty is a Cold War-era arms control agreement that was signed in 1990 by the member states of the Warsaw Pact and NATO. The treaty established limits on the amount of conventional military equipment that countries could have in certain regions of Europe and established a system for inspections and data exchanges to verify compliance with the treaty.

The treaty was seen as an important step towards reducing tensions between the Eastern and Western blocs during the Cold War. However, the treaty has not been ratified by all countries and its implementation has been suspended. The CFE Treaty was suspended in 2007 by Russia, citing the expansion of NATO and the deployment of US missile defense systems in Eastern Europe as reasons for their decision.

Russia also argued that the treaty was no longer valid because the political and military landscape of Europe had changed significantly since the treaty was first signed in 1990.

In addition, Russia did not ratify the Adapted CFE Treaty, which was negotiated in 1999 to take into account the changes in Europe after the collapse of the Soviet Union, and which would have established new limits on military equipment in the region.

Russia's actions led to a dispute with other signatories of the treaty, particularly NATO member states, who argued that

Russia was in violation of the treaty by failing to withdraw its troops from Moldova and Georgia, as required by the treaty. The dispute over the CFE Treaty has contributed to a wider deterioration of relations between Russia and the West in the past decade.[151]

NATO-Russia Council (NRC) 2022

The NATO-Russia Council (NRC) was a mechanism established for the purpose of consulting and consensus-building, cooperation, and joint decision making. The individual NATO member states and Russia worked as equal partners in the area of security issues of common interest. The NRC was established in Rome on May 28, 2002, utilizing the Declaration on "NATO-Russia Relations: a New Quality". The 2002 Rome Declaration, which was developed from the goals and principles of the 1997 NATO-Russia Founding Act on Mutual Relations, Cooperation and Security.[152]

The Partnership for Peace, (1994)

The Partnership for Peace (PfP) is a program established by the North Atlantic Treaty Organization (NATO) in 1994 to promote cooperation and mutual security among European and

---

[151] Daryl Kimball, Gabriela Iveliz Rosa Hernandez The Conventional Armed Forces in Europe (CFE) Treaty and the Adapted CFE Treaty at a Glance https://www.armscontrol.org/factsheet/cfe

[152] NATO (1 September 2022) NATO-Russia Council https://www.nato.int/cps/en/natohq/topics_50091.htm

Euro-Atlantic nations. The program is open to all countries in Europe and the Euro-Atlantic area that are not currently members of NATO, and it provides a framework for these nations to work together with NATO on a wide range of issues, including defense planning, military exercises, and crisis management. The goal of PfP is to build trust and confidence among participating nations, and to promote stability and security in the Euro-Atlantic area.[153]

The Charter for European Security, (1999)

The Charter for European Security, also known as the Tbilisi Charter, is a political declaration adopted by the Organization for Security and Co-operation in Europe, (OSCE) in 1999. The charter is non-binding and outlines the commitment of the OSCE member states to the principles of security, democracy, and human rights in Europe.

The Charter for European Security is considered as a soft law instrument, it is not legally binding, but it is politically and morally binding on countries and is meant to serve as a guide for the actions of the OSCE member states. It was adopted during the OSCE's 1999 Summit in Istanbul and reaffirmed by

---

[153] NATO (30 October 2009) Partnership for Peace: Framework Document https://www.nato.int/cps/en/natolive/official_texts_24469.htm

the OSCE's heads of state and government at the OSCE Summits in Porto and Warsaw.[154]

Provisions of the Manila Declaration on the Peaceful Settlement of International Disputes, (1982)

The Manila Declaration on the Peaceful Settlement of International Disputes is a non-binding resolution adopted by the United Nations General Assembly in 1982. The Declaration reaffirms the principles of the Charter of the United Nations regarding the peaceful settlement of disputes and calls on states to make use of all peaceful means at their disposal to resolve disputes. It is considered a soft law instrument. It is not legally binding, but it is politically and morally binding on countries.[155]

The Washington Treaty, (1949)

The Washington Treaty, also known as the North Atlantic Treaty, is the treaty that established NATO in 1949. The treaty binds its members to mutual defense and cooperation in the event of an armed attack against any member state. It also

---

[154] OSCE (1999) Istanbul Summit
https://www.osce.org/files/f/documents/4/2/17502.pdf

[155] UN Audio Visual Library (15 November 1982) Manila Declaration on the Peaceful Settlement of International Disputes
https://legal.un.org/avl/ha/mdpsid/mdpsid.html

established a council, known as the North Atlantic Council, to oversee the organization and its activities. [156]

NATO'S OFFICIAL RESPONSE TO RUSSIA

The response continues, demanding that the only way NATO will address Russia's concerns is by utilizing a rigid structure of a controlled dialogue architecture. This is to be used to create associative legal instruments through the Strategic Stability Dialogue, (SSD) at the NATO-Russia Council, (NRC) and the OSCE.

NATO demands more information about Russia's classified defensive position and military assets. NATO claims its expansion is justified under the guise of Transparency, Freedom, and Democracy and references the Washington Treaty several times in its response.[157]

"The refusal by the United States on key proposals on security guarantees leads the situation to a dead end."—Deputy Foreign Minister Ryabkov.

---

[156] NATO (2 September 2022) Founding treaty https://www.nato.int/cps/en/natolive/topics_67656.htm

[157] Hibai Arbide Aza, Miguel Gonzalez, El Pais (2 February 2022) US offered disarmament measures to Russia in exchange for deescalation of military threat in Ukraine https://english.elpais.com/usa/2022-02-02/us-offers-disarmament-measures-to-russia-in-exchange-for-a-deescalation-of-military-threat-in-ukraine.html

Russia's Response to the US Response:

Putin says the US response to security guarantees ignores Russia's concerns. Sergei Lavrov, Russia's Ministry of Foreign Affairs, pointed out:

"The United States "twisted" Russia's proposals on security guarantees in the direction of creating advantages for Washington and its allies—ignored the original package of the proposals, choosing topics convenient for itself." [158]

The US reported:

" So what we do is defensive. But when we see this massive Russian military build-up, combined with threatening rhetoric, proposing something which is actually formulated as a kind of ultimatum, that if we don't accept this and that, then there will be, what they call the 'military technical' consequences. And we know the track record of Russia using force against neighbours."

Russia said it will now be forced to respond, including by implementing Military-Technical Measures, in the Absence of the US to negotiate legally binding security guarantees with Russia. The larger conflict between Russia and the US is that both sides have failed to comply with prior agreements; therefore, new instruments were developed. These instruments became so uncompromisingly controlling that Moscow would

---

[158] Tara John, Adrienne Vogt, Melissa Macaya, Maureen Chowdhury (18 February 2022) The latest on the Ukraine-Russia border crisis https://edition.cnn.com/europe/live-news/ukraine-russia-news-02-17-22-intl/h_75663ce67cbe6c9bbff687ae81d9282d

not be able to have any of its security concerns addressed without first compromising its own security and identity.

Later the US response, which was classified, was leaked, and published in the Spanish newspaper El Pais. [159] I can only assume, that if Moscow installed missiles and troops on the US Canadian border, our reaction would be similar.

.

---

[159] El Pais (17 December 2021) Documentos entregados por la OTAN y EE UU en respuesta al tratado que les presentó Rusia el 17 de diciembre de 2021
https://elpais.com/infografias/2022/02/respuesta_otan/respuesta_otan_ee uu.pdf

CHAPTER FIVE

PUTIN RECOGNIZES THE REPUBLICS

The West ignored the atrocities of Ukraine's war on the independent republics of Luhansk and Donetsk for eight years, Putin did not. Instead, he did something about it. On January 30th, 2022, Eduard Basurin, Secretary of the DPR military command, made the statement:

"If supplies of weapons to Kiev continue, Donetsk reserves the right to turn to the Russian Federation and other countries for military and military-technical assistance." [160]

---

[160] Matt Davio (30 January 2022)
https://www.scoopnest.com/user/MissTrade/1488542651955564547-if-supplies-of-weapons-to-kiev-continue-donetsk-reserves-the-right-to-turn-to-the-russian-federatio

UKRAINE STEPS UP ATTACKS

As we have seen, on February 19, 2022, the OSCE reported numerous attacks in the Donbass region. Prior to that we see the reporting of the alleged shelling on the territories of Donetsk and Luhansk, which can't be verified, however the reporting suggests a gradual escalation in attacks from late January to late February.

Though the US calls these reports "False Flags" and "Russian Disinformation," the US State Department and Department of Defense have yet to provide any evidence to prove their allegations are true. They site security concerns and claim they don't want to divulge their source, but as you will see, they monitor the area with spy-planes, and with a high probability of satilites. Certainly, there must be some proof they can show us to defend their claims.

What we do know is:

1. Reports of between 14,000 and 20,000 people died in the Donbass in the last eight years prior to the 2022 Russian invasion. This proves there is a history of attacks between seperatists and Ukraine in the Donbass.

2. The OSCE observed and reported 553 attacks in the Donetsk region on the weekend of the 19th of February 2022.

3. Ukraine received billions of dollars in financial and military assistance one month before the escalation began.

4. On April 2021, the Ukrianian Defense Ministy made the statement saying it had received guarantees of American support after a phone call with Pentagon Chief, Lloyd Austen.[161] After the Russian invasion, NATO and the US said they would not send soldiers into Ukraine to defend her.[162] Afterward President Zelensky made the statement, *"We are left alone in defense of our state..."* as he was seemingly caught by surprise at the lack of support he originally perceived he would get from NATO, which could lead us to speculate that the escalation only occurred because Kiev thought NATO would deploy troops if Russia invaded.

Therefore, it is concievable that allegations of Urkaine stepping up attacks in the region are factual. This would also explain Sergey Naryshkin's statements.

---

[161] Global Security (2021) Russo-Ukraine War – 2021 https://www.globalsecurity.org/military/world/war/russo-ukraine-2021.htm

[162] Paul LeBlanc (28 February 2022) Why the US isn't sending troops into Ukraine https://www.cnn.com/2022/02/27/politics/us-troops-ukraine-russia-what-matters/index.html

Sergey Naryshkin, who serves as the Director of the Foreign Intelligence Service, said:

"Western mentors are pushing Zelensky to finally abandon the Minsk agreements, unleashing a war in Donbass."[163]

An interesting opinion piece by commondreams.org also confirmed that the US encouraged Zelensky to pull back from their commitments of the Minsk Protocol.[164]

Naryshkin also noted that the goal of Kiev was the unleashing of a war in the Donbass to destroy the LNR and the DNR, with an eye to drag Russia into an intra-Ukrainian conflict. Kiev certainly wouldn't have attempted this with Russia without believing NATO would send in troops if Russia invaded.

Vladimir Chizhov, Russian Permanent Representative to the EU, also stated that Russia would not take action against Ukraine if "not provoked to do so."[165]

---

[163] Newizv.ru (21 February 2022) The head of the Foreign Intelligence Service, Sergey Naryshkin, advocated the entry of the DPR and LPR into the Russian Federatio https://en.newizv.ru/news/2022-02-21/the-head-of-the-foreign-intelligence-service-sergey-naryshkin-advocated-the-entry-of-the-dpr-and-lpr-into-the-russian-federation-389420

[164] Medea Benjamin, Nicolas J.S. Davies (8 February 2022) Memo to Congress: Diplomacy for Ukraine Is Spelled M-I-N-S-K https://www.commondreams.org/views/2022/02/08/memo-congress-diplomacy-ukraine-spelled-m-i-n-s-k

[165] Lentra (19 January 2022) Russia promised not to attack Ukraine https://lenta.ru/news/2022/01/19/ryabkovv/

He also added:

"We will respond if Russian citizens are killed anywhere, including in the Donbass."

According to the Minsk 2 agreement, a ceasefire and withdrawal of all heavy weapons were to be removed from the front lines of the Donbass region.[166]

Valerii Zaluzhnyi, the Commander-in-Chief of the Armed Forces of Ukraine, announced that the "command-staff" phase had been completed as part of the "Metel 2022" exercises, a set of practical exercises that began on Wednesday, February 16th, 2022. According to UK Foreign Secretary Truss. Reports of Ukraine's abnormal military activity in the Donbass are a blatant attempt by the Russian government to fabricate pretexts for an invasion.

Reports of heavy shelling by Ukrainian forces could be heard along the front line, in the cities of Spartak and possibly Donetsk City as well.[167] It had been aledged that Ukraine was tired of waiting for the "Russian invasion" and so began

---

[167] Tellerreport (5 February 2022) The Permanent Mission of Russia to the UN condemned the shelling of residential areas in the Donbass by the Armed Forces of Ukraine https://www.tellerreport.com/news/2022-02-05-the-permanent-mission-of-russia-to-the-un-condemned-the-shelling-of-residential-areas-in-the-donbass-by-the-armed-forces-of-ukraine.BkhdNNn0Y.html

escalating its shelling along the entire line of contact in the Donbass as a means of provocation. [168]

It was reported by the DPL that more than two hundred 120-mm mortars had been used against the republics by Ukrainian armed formation.[169] [170] This had been the most active shelling of Ukrainian armed formations in months, according to witnesses. Shelling was executed in at least ten settlements of the republics. Ukraine, at this point, was in violation of its obligations under the ceasefire agreement signed in July of 2020.

The Kremlin noted that senior Ukrainian officials "make contradictory statements." He said:

"On the one hand, Kiev made a statement about its commitment to the Minsk accords. On the other hand, a statement was made that

---

[168] Amos Chapple (26 January 2022) 'Tired Of Waiting': Ukraine Photojournalists Describe Mood On The Front Lines https://www.rferl.org/a/ukraine-front-line-photographers-mood/31670172.html

[169] Intel Slava Z (4 February 2022) https://t.me/intelslava/18055

[170] David Meyer (17 February 2022) Shelling in eastern Ukraine raises tensions even further, as Russian forces continue to mass at the border https://fortune.com/2022/02/17/shelling-eastern-ukraine-luhansk-donetsk-russia-invasion-putin/?_ptid=%7Bkpdx%7DAAAAvgY9CZjzgQoKY2ZRajJmTTN6ahIQb Ghza2MyMGFkb3JpNzgxcxoMRVg1M0lEU01IUVNQIiUxODA1aXI4MG M4LTAwMDAzMjFjcnBsbWVjZm1haDJtdHRyNDQ0KhhzaG93T2ZmZX JUSVdTTIZWNk9RUEIxNDIwAToMT1RYVjIIWNkRMVVI5Qg1PVFYySz VEMEpGTTRRUhJ2LYIA8BhvNDhoZnlzOGNaDTcwLjE4MS4xMzQuND ViA2R3Y2iy1ZujBnAFeAw

the implementation of the Minsk accords would spell the downfall of Ukraine. Moreover, Kiev stated that they would not fulfill the Minsk Agreements on some intangible Russian terms,"[171]

Kiev determined the Minsk agreement was to be used to gain control of its borders. Russia determined the Minsk agreement was going to be used to give autonomy to Donetsk and Luhansk. This difference in prespective gave the Minsk 2 agreements the nickname: "The Minsk Conundrum." [172] On February 8th, 2022, President Emmanuel Macron made the statement that Russia and Ukraine had both committed to hornoring the Minsk Accords, Zelensky reaffirmed by saying:

"Ukraine is committed to fulfilling the Minsk accords, as long as this happens in the way Kyiv interprets them."[173]

---

[171] TASS News (16 February 2022) Putin has ambiguous view of Kiev's willingness to implement Minsk accords — Kremlin https://tass.com/politics/1404561

[172] Aljazeera (9 February 2022) Ukraine-Russia crisis: What is the Minsk agreement? https://www.aljazeera.com/news/2022/2/9/what-is-the-minsk-agreement-and-why-is-it-relevant-now

[173] Shaun Walker (9 February 2022) Can Ukraine and Russia be persuaded to abide by Minsk accords? https://www.theguardian.com/world/2022/feb/09/can-ukraine-and-russia-be-persuaded-to-abide-by-minsk-accords

THE FIRST FALSE FLAG BY UKRAINE

On February 17th, 2022, Christopher Miller wrote on Twitter that, according to local municipal staff and NGO Proliska, an attack occurred at 9 am local, and Russian-backed forces shelled a building in Stani. In the music classroom of a kindergarten in

Figure 17: Map proving the trajectory of the missile was fired into a kindergarten classroom by Ukraine—Courtesy LPR

Stanytsia Luhanska, children were present but were not injured, and two staffers suffered concussions. [174] [175]

The LPR and Kiev blamed each other for the attack,[176] but the LPR reported that the trajectory of the munition used was calculated by the LPR to have been shot from the east side of the Siverskyi Donets River, where Ukrainian forces had a stronghold at the time.

There were critics trying to discount the story as Russian disinformation by photoshopping the image—placing a pneumatic drill beside the school but the author of the post admitted it was fake. As the war raged on over time, Ukraine would falsely accuse Russia of many such attacks, and were all debunked publicly by the US and EU.

The Luhansk People's Republic claimed the map shown above proves the shelling of the kindergarten class was a false flag attack perpetrated by the Ukraine Army. It shows the

---

[174] Christopher Miller
https://twitter.com/ChristopherJM/status/1494232112328843265

[175] HRW (18 February 2022) Ukraine: Shelling Residential Areas Puts Civilians at Risk https://www.hrw.org/news/2022/02/18/ukraine-shelling-residential-areas-puts-civilians-risk

[176] Haley Ott, Tucker Reals (17 February 2022) U.S. says Russia moving toward "imminent invasion" of Ukraine amid "false-flag" concerns over shelling claims in Donbas https://www.cbsnews.com/news/russia-ukraine-news-donbas-rebels-shelling-putin-response-us-proposals/

location where the munition was fired from, two km Southeast of the classroom. *(See figure 17 above)*

One source reported that a mortor that hit the school yard was estimated to have been launched from the southern controlled separatist areas, however, the projectile that hit the classroom clearly was not launched from the same direction.

It is alleged that Armed Forces of Ukraine continued the massive shelling of the city. Among other objects, the buildings of School No. 105 in the Petrovsky district and School No. 56 in the Kievsky district were seriously damaged.

Reuters reported the incident could not be verified, but initial reports suggested that the attacks, which government forces and pro-Russians had accused of each other, were similar in scale to ceasefire violations common between the two sides during the eight-year conflict. [177]

Another False flag, this time, to favor the DPR, was set up to look like a car bombing involving 3 victims. An IDE apparently exploded causing the 3 victims to parish in the fire. Upon further examinations, it was concluded by experts that the vehicle

---

[177] Reuters (17 February 2022) Russian-backed Ukraine rebels accuse government forces of mortar attack
https://www.reuters.com/world/europe/ukraine-rebels-accuse-govt-forces-mortar-shelling-report-2022-02-17/

appeared to be struck by gun fire, rather than an IDE, and there was no indentation on the side that the IDE apparently struck.

The victims were also examined, and one of which had clear lacerated by a bone saw, to the front of the skull in the same manner that would take place in an autopsy. It was revealed that the vehicle itself was not in motion at the time of the explosion on the highway. All of this concluded that someone acquired 3 cadavers and placed them in a vehicle and set them on fire to look like the vehicle was attacked by an IDE. No references to the incident are listed due to the graphic nature of the photos.

The AFP reported that the UN urges 'restraint' by all parties amid reports of fresh shelling in eastern Ukraine. [178] The Ukrainian military denied accusations of shelling settlements in the Donbass and said that they are complying with the Minsk agreements. We know this now to be completely false. Both sides have continued to do battle with one another throughout the entire eight years since the referendums of the LPR and DPR, during which the hostilities began. But we also know by the map shown below, the shelling has increased exponentially, as confirmed by multiple eyewitnesses and the DPR.

---

[178] The Times of Israel UN urges 'restraint' by all parties amid fresh shelling in eastern Ukraine
https://www.timesofisrael.com/liveblog_entry/un-urges-restraint-by-all-parties-amid-fresh-shelling-in-eastern-ukraine/

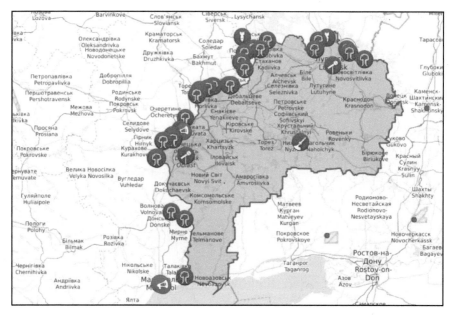

Figure 18: Shelling of the Donbass by Ukrainian forces increased exponentially just before the start of the war--Courtesy Bellum Acta.

Denis Pushilin, the head of Donetsk People's Republic said:

"Zelensky will soon give the order to the military to launch an offensive in the Donbass, to implement a plan to invade the territory of the DPR and LPR."[179]

---

[179] Tellerreport.com (18 February 2022) The head of the DPR Pushilin: Zelensky will soon order to go on the offensive in the Donbass https://www.tellerreport.com/news/2022-02-18-the-head-of-the-dpr-pushilin—zelensky-will-soon-order-to-go-on-the-offensive-in-the-donbass.HyHWLyXp1c.html

The head of the LPR, Leonid Pasechnik, signed a decree that would begin the mobilization of citizens to register for the military and prepare for battle. [180]

On February 18th, 2022, an explosion in Donetsk thundered a few dozen meters from the government building of the DPR, RIA Novosti correspondent reports. A military vehicle belonging to Denis Sinenkov, the Major General of the Donetsk People's Republic was alleged to be a failed assassination attempt.[181] It didn't take long for the US State Department to announce that this may be a pretext for a Russian invasion.

---

[180] Jonathan Brown, AFP (19 February 2022) Ukraine Rebel Leaders Announce 'General Mobilization' https://www.themoscowtimes.com/2022/02/19/ukraine-rebel-leaders-announce-general-mobilization-a76465

[181] TASS News (18 February 2022) Car that blew up in Donetsk belongs to militia official — report https://tass.com/emergencies/1406225

THE STAKES GET HIGHER

Russian Foreign Ministry said, "a genocide by Kiev" is underway in Donbass, but Western media where quick to call them "baseless", and "ridiculous", while they themselves quoted US officials who also did not present evidence to the contrary.

In one article by the Business Insider: *"Russian President Vladimir Putin on Tuesday claimed, without evidence, that 'genocide' is occurring..."*[182]

The OSCE, however, reported that there were 975 ceasefire violations in the Luhansk region including 860 explosions.[183] The OSCE was able to differentiate between heavy artillary, explosives, and small arms fire, but failed to provide the location of the "origin" of the heavy artillary activity.

At this time, it was apparent that President Putin had begun to execute his plan for a "Special military operation" against Ukraine.

---

[182] John Haltiwanger (15 February 2022) Putin baselessly claims 'genocide' is happening in areas of Ukraine controlled by Kremlin-backed rebels https://www.businessinsider.com/putin-claims-genocide-happening-in-donbas-region-of-ukraine-2022-2

[183] OSCE (19 February 2022) OSCE Special Monitoring Mission to Ukraine (SMM) Daily Report 39/2022 issued on 19 February 2022 https://www.osce.org/special-monitoring-mission-to-ukraine/512629

Igor Guskov, the First Deputy Governor of the Rostov region, received five billion rubles from the Russian federal budget. This was allocated to help the evacuated residents of the Donetsk and Luhansk People's Republics:

"They were brought to the Ministry of Labor of the Rostov Region, ten thousand each for payments to citizens. On Saturday, when registering, we will be able to start paying out these funds in this order." [184]

Trains are also starting to transport refugees from the DPR to the Rostov region.

Alexander Chupriyan, Acting Head of the Ministry of Emergency Situations of the Russian Federation, said:

"The train will start working on Saturday. Each train consists of ten wagons, capacity—900 people"

Russian media sources posted videos and photos of mass mobilization and evacuation of civilians by Russia from the

---

[184] Pravda News (18 February 2022) Russia readies for war as Donbass evacuates population https://english.pravda.ru/news/hotspots/150373-russia_donbass/

Donbass on Telegram.[185][186][187][188][189] Viktor Vodolatsky, the First Deputy Chairman of the State Duma Committee on CIS Affairs, announced that the first 45 buses from the Donbass entered the Rostov region. Women, children, and the elderly were first to be evacuated from Donetsk to Russia. By February 20th, 2022, 61,000 pro-Russian citizens from the Donbass had crossed the Russian border into Russia according to Aleksandr Chupriyan, Miniser of Emergency Situations, Russian Federation.[190] By February 23rd, 91,000 refugees from the LPR and DPR will have crossed the Russian border.

On February 18th, the US accused Russia's military intelligence directorate, or GRU, for distributed denial-of-service (DDoS) against the ministry of Ukriane, and Ukraine's

---

[185] DW (18 February 2022) Separatists in Donetsk evacuate civilians https://www.dw.com/en/separatists-in-donetsk-evacuate-civilians/video-60838023

[186] TASS News (18 February 2022) Donetsk, Lugansk republics announce evacuations of civilians amid Donbass escalation https://tass.com/world/1406155

[187] Intel Slava Z (18 February 2022) https://t.me/intelslava/18920

[188] Intel Slava Z (18 February 2022) https://t.me/intelslava/18925

[189] Intel Slava Z (18 February 2022) https://t.me/intelslava/18929

[190] Intel Slava Z (20 February 2022) https://t.me/intelslava/19275

banking institutions.[191] Ukraine's Military Defense Intelligence announced on Twitter:

"The Public Relations Service of the Ministry of Defense of Ukraine is authorized to state that Ukraine's military intelligence has information about the undermining of a number of social infrastructure facilities in Donetsk by Russian special services in order to further undermine them." [192]

In a show of military might, President Putin oversaw their military strategic deterrence drills on February 19th, 2022, which included ballistic and cruise missile launches.[193]

By February 20th, 2022, the OSCE had logged 2,000 ceasefire violations in Eastern Ukraine.[194] Special Representative of the OSCE Chairmanship in Ukraine called the situation in

---

[191] Morgan Chalfant (18 February 2022) White House says Russia behind cyberattack on banks, ministry in Ukraine https://thehill.com/policy/cybersecurity/594947-white-house-says-russia-behind-cyberattack-on-banks-in-ukraine/

[192] Aggelos Chorianopoulos... (18 February 2022) https://twitter.com/search?q=The%20Public%20Relations%20Service%20of%20the%20Ministry%20of%20Defense%20of%20Ukraine%20is%20authorized%20to%20state%20that%20Ukraine%E2%80%99s%20military%20&src=typeahead_click

[193] DW (19 February 2022) Putin presides over Russian missile drills https://www.dw.com/en/vladimir-putin-presides-over-russian-missile-drills/a-60831388

[194] Anton Zverev, Tom Balmforth, Matthew Lewis (20 February 2022) Almost 2,000 ceasefire violations logged in eastern Ukraine -diplomatic source https://www.reuters.com/world/europe/almost-2000-ceasefire-violations-logged-eastern-ukraine-diplomatic-source-2022-02-19/

Donbass "very alarming."[195] Ukrainian Military Intelligence Agency accused Russian Special Forces of placing explosives in the city of Donetsk and urged people to stay inside and not to use public transportation.[196] The OSCE continued to remain silent as to where the attacks were coming from.

At this point the Minsk agreements null and void. The UN called for an immediate ceasefire in eastern Ukraine and to practice maximum restraint.

The White House press pool reported that Joe Biden held a telephone conversation with the leaders of NATO which included: Romania, Poland, France, Italy, Germany, Great Britain, Canada, and the European Union officials. The conversation began at 2:45 pm Washington DC time. The topic of contact is the situation around Ukraine.

President Vladimir Putin signed a decree that day calling up Russians in reserve for military training. This is an annual event, but Biden took this as a threat to Ukraine.

At midnight Saturday, February 19th, 2022, Jen Psaki issued the following statement on the situation in Ukraine:

---

[195] TRT World News, AFP (19 February 2022) Reports show 'dramatic increase' in Ukraine ceasefire violations – OSCE https://www.trtworld.com/europe/reports-show-dramatic-increase-in-ukraine-ceasefire-violations-osce-54907

[196] VOI (19 February 2022) Ukraine Says Russian Troops Installed Explosives At Donetsk Fasilitas Facility https://voi.id/en/news/136770

"...Biden continues to monitor the evolving situation in Ukraine, and is being updated regularly about events on the ground by his national security team. They reaffirmed that Russia could launch an attack against Ukraine at any time."[197]

Eyewitnesses reported on social networks that the gas pipeline was on fire and that there were also terrorist attacks in the city of Luhansk. The explosion of the gas pipeline in the capital of the LPR was also attributed to a terrorist attack by the Kiev regime on the Donbass republics. This was reported by Andrey Rudenko, the military commander of Luhansk.[198] [199]

Russian special military operations were said to be seen in the Donbass region. It was reported that the damage that caused both explosions on the gas pipeline turned out to be sabotage. At 9 am on February 19th, 2022, Russia's forces in the area reported 19 violations of the ceasefire agreement was recorded.

[197] White House Press Briefing (19 February 2022) Statement from Press Secretary Jen Psaki on President Biden's Briefings on Ukraine https://www.whitehouse.gov/briefing-room/statements-releases/2022/02/19/statement-from-press-secretary-jen-psaki-on-president-bidens-briefings-on-ukraine/

[198] Reuters (19 February 2022) Russian gas exports to Europe not affected by eastern Ukraine pipeline blast https://www.reuters.com/world/europe/gas-pipeline-ukraines-breakaway-region-catches-fire-after-blast-reports-2022-02-18/

[199] Andrey Ostroukh, Natalia Zinets, Katya Golubkova, Chris Reese, Jane Merriman (19 February 2022) Russian gas exports to Europe not affected by eastern Ukraine pipeline blast https://www.reuters.com/world/europe/gas-pipeline-ukraines-breakaway-region-catches-fire-after-blast-reports-2022-02-18/

Russia heightened tensions with a report that Putin initiated Hypersonic Missile drills in the Mediterranean Sea from the coast of Syria.

The Border Service of the Federal Security Service— Russian Federation (FSB) Confirms two shells landed on Russian territory. Ukraine denied the firing of shells that fell in Russia and called for an international investigation.

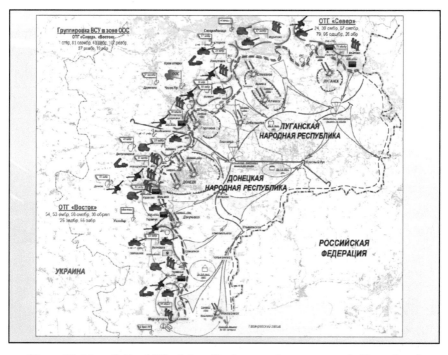

Figure 19: Map of alleged Ukrainian offensive operation to overrun the Donetsk and Luhansk Republics February 2022--Courtesy DPR

Regions of settlements in the north and south of the Donetsk People's Republic were subjected to massive strikes from the Ukrainian troops, the DPR representative office in the JCCC alleged. It is important to note that the JCCC was the Joint Centre of Control and Coordination, who's was a group of Ukrainiand and Russian officers, who's purpose was to monitor ceasefire violations, similar to the OSCE. The JCCC disbanded in 2017 according to Wikipedia, however, members of the Russian forces still wear the old uniforms when reporting these recent violations. [200]

Sputnik News Agency reported that a Ukrainian Intelligence agent involved in the car bombing and attempted assasination in Central Donetsk was apprehended and detained by Separatist Authorities.

There were 63 incidents of shelling that had reportedly taken place in the direction of populated villages and settlements. Those targeted were Grigorovka, Kamenka, Styla, Belaya, and Zaitsevo.

Military Defense Intelligence of Ukraine announced on Twitter:

---

[200] Wikipedia (2023) Joint Centre of Control and Coordination
https://en.wikipedia.org/wiki/Joint_Centre_of_Control_and_Coordination

"These measures are aimed at destabilizing the situation in the temporarily occupied territories of our state and create grounds for accusing Ukraine of terrorist attacks."[201]

Tracers were flying over Donetsk, and the sounds of battles were heard on the outskirts of the city. It was reported that a Ukrainian drone was shot down by anti-aircraft guns in the city of Donetsk. Two civilians were killed in the shelling of the Pionerskoe village by the Armed Forces of Ukraine. The People's Republic returned fire.

UKRAINIAN CITIZENS PREPARE FOR WAR

On the Western side of Ukraine, an American who goes by the name of "Adam" from South Carolina joined the Georgia National Legion to help train Ukraine Civilians "amid escalation from Russia." He said:

"They are preparing for war, it's also very inspiring that they are willing to do so."

---

[201] Savastian Hughes (18 February 2022) Ukraine Accuses Russia Of Rigging Explosives To Manufacture Terrorist Attack https://dailycaller.com/2022/02/18/ukraine-russia-terrorist-attack-explosives-false-flag/

The Polish Ministry of Defense announced that US Military personnel stationed in Poland conducted exercises near the Ukrainian border.

US Embassy sent warnings of possible terrorist attacks in Russia. On February 21st, 2022, at about 6 am Moscow time, the Russian FSB and the Southern Military District border patrol prevented entry of a Ukrainian reconnaissance and sabotage group through the Russian border in the area of Mityakinskaya, Rostov oblast. Two infantry fighting vehicles belonging to the Armed Forces of Ukraine were able to cross the border of the Russian Federation during the clash.

Five members of the Ukrainian Armed Forces were destroyed, along with both infantry vehicles, after a unit of the Russian Armed Forces destroyed the units with anti-tank

weapons. No Russian servicemen or border guards were injured.
202

There was a US sent a spy plane flying along the Ukrainian
Russian border observing the sabotage of munitions by Ukraine

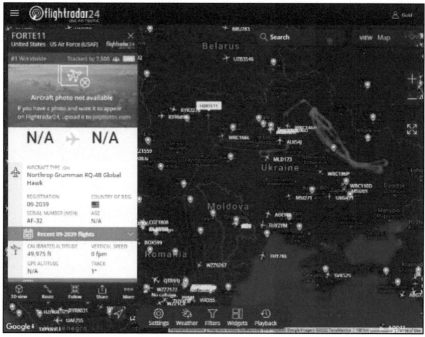

Figure 22: FlightRadar24 captures US spy plane flying near Ukraine Russian border--
Courtesy FlightRadar24

Special Forces. The US called it a "false flag", but a FlightRadar24
radar map was posted showing the US was recorded flying along

202 Emily Crane (21 February 2022) Russia kills 5 'Ukrainian saboteurs'
allegedly trying to breach border: report
https://nypost.com/2022/02/21/russia-kills-5-ukrainian-saboteurs-
allegedly-trying-to-breach-border/

the Ukrainian Russian border. In fact, FlightRadar24 told reporters that Fortell, a US spy plane was its most watched flight.[203] This is also highly likely considering the US has flown missions over Eastern Ukraine previously.[204]

The Armed Forces of Ukraine deliberately targeted an electrical substation in the Petrovsky district of the Donetsk region. RIA Novosti reported that a state-level emergency had been declared due to the shutdown of the pumping station at the South Donbass water pipeline; over 21,000 people and 50 social facilities were without drinking water.[205]

---

[203] Tom Sims, Miranda Murray, Angus MacSwan (21 February 2022) U.S. Air Force spy plane takes spotlight in empty Ukraine airspace https://www.reuters.com/business/aerospace-defense/us-air-force-spy-plane-takes-spotlight-empty-ukraine-airspace-2022-02-22/

[204] Barbara Starr (29 December, 2021) US flies reconnaissance aircraft over eastern Ukraine https://www.cnn.com/2021/12/29/politics/us-reconnaissance-aircraft-ukraine/index.html

[205] Tellerreport, Russiart, RIA Novosti (21 February 2022) RIA Novosti: shelling is underway in the area of Donetsk airport https://www.tellerreport.com/news/2022-02-21-ria-novosti—shelling-is-underway-in-the-area-of-%E2%80%8B%E2%80%8Bdonetsk-airport.SkfyBZGZgq.html

RUSSIA RECOGNIZES THE LPR AND DPR AS INDEPENDENT REPUBLICS

On February 21st, 2022, Eduard Basurin, the head of the Donetsk Peaple's Republic officially announced the need to receive assistance from the Russian Federation. Russia's State Duma Speaker Vyacheslav Volodin announced:

"We officially ask the President of Russian Federation Vladimir Putin to consider the appeal of the State Duma and recognize the LPR and the DPR as independent countries."[206]

Russia recognizing the Separatist Republics in Eastern Ukraine not only implies that the regions are now a separate country from Ukraine but also implies that Russia also recognized their sovereignty, including areas controlled by Ukraine such as Mariupol, home to the Nationalist Azov battalion, Kramatorsk, Sloviansk, and many others. Estonian Foreign Ministry called on the EU to impose sanctions against Russia in case of recognition of the DPR and LPR.

According to NATO Secretary General Stoltenberg, If Russia recognizes the DPR and LPR, it will violate international law and complicate the settlement under the Minsk agreements. Nine of the twelve members of the Russian Security Council,

---

[206] BBC News (21 February 2022) The leaders of the DPR and LPR asked Putin to recognize them as states
https://www.bbc.com/russian/news-60465863 (Russian)

including Sergey Lavrov and Sergey Shoigu, have recommended the immediate recognition of the Donetsk and Luhansk republics. In an interesting overzealous statement, or perhaps a Freudian slip, Sergey Naryshkin, a member of President Putin's security council, stated:

"I support the annexation of the Donetsk and Luhansk republics to the Russian Federation."

President Putin responded:

"We are not discussing this."[207]

President Putin also proclaimed:

"The Ukrainian authorities are not going to implement the Minsk agreements."

Kozak agreed with him.

Then Putin said:

"With the usual development of events will not be. They will never be."[208]

On the morning of February 21st, 2022, Moscow time, it was announced that Vladimir Putin was to recognize the Eastern

---

[207] BBC News (21 February 2022) The leaders of the DPR and LPR asked Putin to recognize them as states https://www.bbc.com/russian/news-60465863 (Russian)

[208] BBC News (Russian) (21 February 2022) "The decision will be made. Today". Russian Security Council discussed recognition of DPR and LPR https://www.bbc.com/russian/news-60465864

Ukraine Separatist Republics of Luhansk and Donetsk as independent States.

After Russia recognizes the Donbass republics, the respective borders of the DPR and LPR would need to be defined by the documents on sovereignty and confirmed by the referendum held in 2014. From the point of view of the LPR and the DPR, the territories which are now under the control of the Armed Forces of Ukraine are considered occupiers.

Figure 21: President Putin signs decree recognizing the republics of the DLR and PLR-- Courtesy Russia Today.

President Putin made a comprehensive speech that lasted nearly an hour on the history of the Donbass and how this particular region was a part of Russia. He spoke on the coup of the President of Ukraine in 2014, and the resistance of Ukrainian

"Nationalism" by the Donetsk Peoples Republic and Luhansk Peoples Republic.

President Putin also mentioned Ukraine's "Nazism" and "Russophobia" and said, "It [recognition of the LPR and DPR] should have been done long ago." Vladimir Putin then asked the Federal Assembly of Russia to support and rectify his decision. With that, President Putin signed a decree on live TV to recognize the two breakaway republics as independent states, along with representatives of the republics.

THE DONBASS CELEBRATES

Figure 22: Sergey Aksyonov, Governor of Crimea celebrates the recognition of the republics -- Courtesy rk.gov.ru

February 21st, 2022, Citizens began gathering in Donetsk city to listen to President Putin's announcement that Russia will recognize DPR and LPR as independent. The people anxiously wait to celebrate. This day may go down in history as the day the Donbass war ended. The Minsk Agreements were officially gone and will also be recognized as a complete failure—its provisions were never fully realized.[209]

Venezuela, Cuba, Syria, North Korea, South Ossetia, Abkhazia, Belarus, Central African Republic, Nicaragua, Sudan, Artsakh, and Chechnya also recognize the Donetsk and Luhansk republics. The head of Chechnya, Ramzan Kadyrov, said he fully supports the decision to recognize the DPR and LPR.[210]

Moscow signed a mutual security agreement with the LPR and DPR that entails provisions for mutual protection.

Putin:

"We demand from those who seized and held power in Kiev to immediately stop hostilities or face consequences."[211]

The heads of the European Commission as well as the European Council called Moscow's recognition of the DPR and

[209] Wikipedia (2022) Minsk agreements
https://en.wikipedia.org/wiki/Minsk_agreements

[210] Wikipedia (2022) International recognition of the Donetsk People's Republic and the Luhansk People's Republic
https://en.wikipedia.org/wiki/International_recognition_of_the_Donetsk_People%27s_Republic_and_the_Luhansk_People%27s_Republic

[211] TASS News (21 February 2022) Recognition of Donbass and warning to Kiev — Putin's address to nation https://tass.com/politics/1407811

LPR as independent constitutes a violation of international law and the Territorial Integrity of Ukraine.[212]

Russia's Ambassador to the UN, Vasily Nebenzya argued for the need to defend the republics in eastern Ukraine's Donbass region from Ukrainian aggression:

"Allowing a new bloodbath in the Donbass is something we do not intend to do."[213]

Mr. Biden signed an executive order targeting investment, trade, and financing, which prohibited US citizens from providing any form of financial support to the Donetsk and Luhansk republics. Citizens in many parts of the Donbass report that the situation is calm, with no shelling. The separatist militaries also had no report of ceasefire violations since Putin's speech.

---

[212] BBC (Russian) (21 February 2022) Putin in a televised address to Russia announced recognition of the DPR and LPR https://www.bbc.com/russian/news-60466414

[213] BBC (22 February 2022) Ukraine crisis: Russia orders troops into rebel-held regions https://www.bbc.com/news/world-europe-60468237

Figure 23: Donetsk patriotically fly DPR flags throughout the territory--Courtesy korupciya.com

European officials told Western agencies that the EU decided it will not impose sanctions against Russia due to the recognition of the DPR and LPR until after they see what Moscow will do next. The Ukrainian security council meeting about Ukraine's next steps was postponed indefinitely. Apparently, Zelensky was so discombobulated about the event he reportedly could not come to a decision on what to do.

Zelensky had telephone conferences with Joe Biden, the UK and EU, and would have found out that the US, nor their NATO allies would be sending troops into Ukraine to help fight. Joe

Biden urged Zelensky to use Diplomacy and deterrence to resolve the threat. [214]

Protests broke out in Washington, DC in support of the Donetsk and Luhansk Peoples Republics. The Russian Defense

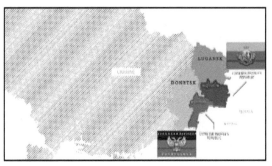

Ministry announced that Russia would take all available measures to eliminate the threat to peace in the Donbass.

Figure 24: Occupied territories map-Donbass--Courtesy Bellum Acta

The Donbass news agency, "Defenders of the Donbass" reported:

"While being recognized by the Motherland was a great victory, there is still work to be done. All the grey land you see on this map is Ukrainian occupied land. It must be liberated."[215]

---

[214] Bellum Acta (21 February 2022) https://t.me/BellumActaNews/70622

[215] Defenders of the Donbass (21 February 2022) https://t.me/svobodadonbass/280

THE DENAZIFICATION AND DEMILITARIZATION OF UKRAINE

On February 23rd, 2022, President Putin outlined the country's "Special military operation" in Ukraine, including the 'demilitarization' and 'denazification' of Ukraine. [216]

The Svoboda party, which is one of the more prominent parties in Ukraine, has ties to the Ukrainian partisan party in World War II, which aligned with Nazi Germany. The Svoboda was called the Social-National Party until 2004, which was a deliberate reference to the Nazi's National-Socialist Party. Oleh Tyahnybok, the leader of the Svoboda party, has openly targeted Jews and ethnic Russians in Ukraine for many years.

In 2004, Oleh Tyahnybok made a speech where he called for Ukrainians to fight against a "Muscovite-Jewish mafia." He was kicked out of Viktor Yushenko's government soon after. In 2005, he wrote letters demanding Ukraine put an end to the "criminal activities" of "organized Jewry."[217]

---

[216] ABC News (23 February 2022) Russia announces military operation in Ukraine https://abcnews.go.com/International/video/russia-announces-military-operation-ukraine-83075520

[217] Wikipedia (2019) Svoboda (political party) https://en.wikipedia.org/wiki/Svoboda_(political_party)

Many in the media reported the rise of Nazism in Ukraine until the tensions between Ukraine and Russia escalated in 2020. Here are just of few articles published after 2014, but before February 2022:

"Ukraine celebrates Nazi collaborator, bans book critical of pogroms leader" –TimesOfIsrael.com, December 27, 2018

"Ukraine's got a real problem with far-right violence (And no, RT didn't write this headline)" –Atlantic Council: June 20, 2018

"Hundreds march in Ukraine in annual tribute to Nazi collaborator" –TimesOfIsrael.com, January 4, 2021:

"Ukraine conflict: 'White power' warrior from Sweden" –BBC, July 16, 2014

"Who Was Stepan Bandera?" –HistoryNewsNetwork.org, 2015

"Ukraine: Far-Right Fighters from Europe Fight for Ukraine"— Eurasianet.org, August 6, 2014

"Nazi symbols, salutes on display at Ukrainian nationalist march" –TimesOfIsrael.com, April 30, 2018

"Kiev's far-right groups refuse to disarm"—France 24, March 4, 2014

The European Parliament, also recognizing the growing popularity of Nazism in Ukraine, passed a resolution in 2012, declaring the Svoboda party as "racist, anti-Semitic and xenophobic."[218]

Every January 1st, tens of thousands of Svoboda followers march through the streets of Ukraine, holding torches to honor the birth of Stepan Bandera, the leader of the Ukrainian partisan forces who sided with Nazi Germany during the Second World War.[219]

When Yatsenyuk became Prime Minister in 2014, he rewarded Svoboda's role in the coup by appointing three cabinet positions, including Oleksander Sych as Deputy Prime Minister and three of Ukraine's twenty-five provinces the governorship. Svoboda's Andriy Parubiy was appointed Chairman of Parliament and would hold that position for five years.[220]

Ukraine's Azov battalion, which was more popularly known as "The Militia" was trained by the United States, after Crimea was Annexed into Russia in 2014. The Azov battalion was

---

[218] David Speedie (6 March 2014) Rein in Ukraine's neo-fascists https://www.cnn.com/2014/03/06/opinion/speedie-ukraine-far-right/index.html

[219] Jason Lemon (27 December 2018) Ukraine Makes Birthday of Nazi Collaborator a National Holiday and Bans Book Critical of Anti-Semitic Leader https://www.newsweek.com/ukraine-nazi-collaborator-birthday-holiday-anti-semitic-1272911

[220] Wikipedia (2020) Andriy Parubiy https://en.wikipedia.org/wiki/Andriy_Parubiy

founded by Andriy Biletsky, an avowed white supremacist.[221] [222] He claimed the purpose of the Azov was to rid Ukraine of Jews and other inferior races.[223] [224]

Far-Right mercenaries claimed that they specifically joined Azov because of their affiliation with the far-right.[225] Azov patches have been rebranded slightly but still include the Nazi-linked Wolfsangel symbol and Black Sun Nazi designs. Several captured Azov troops had Swastika tattoos. In a tweet by Ukraine's National Guard posted a video showing Azov fighters

[221] Wikipedia (2020) Andriy Biletsky
https://en.wikipedia.org/wiki/Andriy_Biletsky

[222] Lev Golinkin (22 February 2019) Neo-Nazis and the Far Right Are On the March in Ukraine https://www.thenation.com/article/politics/neo-nazis-far-right-ukraine/

[223] Allan Ripp (5 March 2022) Ukraine's Nazi problem is real, even if Putin's 'denazification' claim isn't https://www.nbcnews.com/think/opinion/ukraine-has-nazi-problem-vladimir-putin-s-denazification-claim-war-ncna1290946

[224] Stanford (2022) Azov Movement
https://cisac.fsi.stanford.edu/mappingmilitants/profiles/azov-battalion

[225] AlJazeera (1 March 2022) Profile: Who are Ukraine's far-right Azov regiment? https://www.aljazeera.com/news/2022/3/1/who-are-the-azov-regiment

coating their bullets in pig fat to be used against Muslim Chechen fighters, fighting for Russia.[226]

Since February 2022, Mainstream Media, the US State Department, and the Pentagon all claim Vladimir Putin created a false narrative about 'Nazis' in Ukraine, committing genocide, to justify his invasion.[227]

Figure 25: Captured Nazi soldier from the AZOV battalion--Courtesy Konkretno.ru

Multiple news agencies confirmed that the US intelligence had issued a new warning to the Ukrainian government that a full-scale attack by Russia was imminent. A citizen of Avdeevka told reporters,

---

[226] Aljazeera (28 February 2022) Ukrainian fighters grease bullets against Chechens with pig fat.
https://www.aljazeera.com/news/2022/2/28/ukrainian-fighters-grease-bullets-against-chechens-with-pig-fat

[227] Rachel Treisman (1 March 2022) Putin's claim of fighting against Ukraine 'neo-Nazis' distorts history, scholars say
https://www.npr.org/2022/03/01/1083677765/putin-denazify-ukraine-russia-history

"We believe we'll be with you soon. All of the Donbass will be united, and we'll greet the Russians with flowers."[228]

On April 11th, 2022, Zelensky addressed the Greek Parliament, and the left-wing lawmakers walked out of the speech for including two neo-Nazi Azov batallion members in the presentation, one of which tweeting:

"The speech of the members of the neo-Nazi Order Azov in the Greek Parliament is a challenge. The absolute responsibility lies with the University. He talked about a historic day but it is a historical shame. Solidarity with the Ukrainian people is a given, but the Nazis can not have a say in Parliament." [229]

When Zelensky was asked in an interview with Western media regarding the Azov battalion and its Nazi affiliation being engaged in carrying out war crimes, he admitted it was true by stating, "They are what they are." [230]

---

[228] CIG, Telegram (2/22/2022) https://t.me/CIG_telegram/16805

[229] Kim Iversen, Robby Soave (11 April 2022) https://www.youtube.com/watch?v=F0tAWaNEhU8&t=1s

[230] Breaking Points (5 April 2022) Fox News CONFRONTS Zelensky On Ukraine Neo-Nazi Battalion | Breaking Points with Krystal and Saagar https://www.youtube.com/watch?v=yGiNzgxeoNk

CHAPTER SIX

INVASION Z-FORCE

The Independent Republics of Donetsk and Luhansk had been under attack by Kiev for over eight years and killed between 14,000 to 20,000 of its citizens. Though the UN expressed concern and advised both sides to respect international humanitarian law, it did not condemn Ukraine.

Now the LPR and DPR have become recognized as independent, and Russia, its greatest ally, vowed to protect the Donbass from Kiev, but not just by guarding the territories of the independent republics but by taking out all of Ukraine's military and NAZI-affiliated leadership.

TANKS AND TROOPS ENTER THE DONBASS

The first units of the Russian Armed Forces entered the DPR and LPR on February 21st, 2022, as peacekeepers,[231] but a larger contingency of Russian troops would move into the region on the front lines with Ukraine on February 24th, 2022.[232] We also know that Russian Special Forces were stationed in the Donbass region on February 18th, 2022.

The Russian Defense Ministry announced that Russia would take all available measures to eliminate the threat of peace in the Donbass. They also assured the public that the civilian population of Ukraine would not be purposely targeted unless they had become armed combatants.[233] As it happened, 8 civilians were allegedly killed according to Kiev, but later it will be revealed how the AFU used civilians as human shields and

[231] BBC News (22 February 2022) Ukraine crisis: Russia orders troops into rebel-held regions https://www.bbc.com/news/world-europe-60468237

[232] Aljazeera (24 February 2022) Why is Russia attacking Ukraine? What we know so far https://www.aljazeera.com/news/2022/2/24/explainer-russias-invasion-of-ukraine-what-we-know-so-far

[233] Aljazeera (24 February 2022) Kyiv says 8 killed; Moscow says not targeting Ukraine cities https://www.aljazeera.com/news/2022/2/24/russia-says-not-targeting-ukraine-cities-kyiv-claims-8-killed

hid heavy artillary in and around civilian neighborhoods. Ukraine's allegations could not be verified.

Ukraine soldiers began receiving text messages that Russia was going to defeat their Army in two days.

Figure 26: The first day of attacks against Ukraine—Courtesy Intel Slava Z

Vladimir Putin instructed the Russian forces to preserve the peace in the DPR and LPR from the Ukrainian military. Russian warplanes flew over Ukraine and began bombing critical military and air facilities.

The Russian Defense Ministry reported that high-precision weapons disabled military bases, air defense facilities, military airfields, and aviation in Chuguev and Galicia, Kharkov, and the Sumy region. In addition, the Russian Defense Ministry reported that high-precision weapons disabled the military infrastructure, air defense facility, and air and aviation of the Ukrainian Army.[234]

Cyber attacks were also being conducted against the Security Services of Ukraine. The Ministry of Defense reported Problems with Internet access at Ukrainian banks, and their ATMs. The website of the Ministry of Defense mil.gov.ua and Armed Forces zsu.gov.ua were also down. Problems were reported with the State Bank, Oschadbank, and Privatbank. ATMs in areas of Mariupol that were controlled by the Ukrainian Army ran out of cash in hours. Locals continued to withdraw their money from banks in the area throughout the day.[235]

When the bombing began, the White House reported that under no circumstances would the United States send troops to Ukraine to fight with Russia.[236] Likewise, Jens Stoltenberg, NATO Secretary General, also announced they had no plans or

---

[234] Joseph P Chacko (24 February 2022) Russia disabled Ukranian military infrastructure with precision strikes, civilians safe https://frontierindia.com/russia-disabled-ukranian-military-infrastructure-with-precision-strikes-civilians-safe/

[235] Joe Tidy, BBC (24 February 2022) Ukraine crisis: 'Wiper' discovered in latest cyber-attacks https://www.bbc.com/news/technology-60500618

[236] Vivian Salama (24 February 2022) White House Says No Plan to Send U.S. Troops to Ukraine https://www.wsj.com/livecoverage/russia-ukraine-latest-news-2022-04-19/card/white-house-says-no-plan-to-send-u-s-troops-to-ukraine-MBoyRzWLmVoNflBNvvrU

intentions of deploying NATO troops to Ukraine. [237] News agencies in the West reported Joe Biden would be announcing "Full-Scale Sanctions" on Russia. Canada began evacuating members of its embassy to Poland.

The next day, President Zelensky proclaimed:

"We are left alone in defense of our state. Who is ready to fight with us? I don't see it. Who is ready to guarantee Ukraine's accession to NATO? Everyone is afraid."[238]

KA-52 helicopters were seen flying at low altitudes, just over the roof lines of buildings in Crimea. Russian tanks were observed just outside of the city of Kharkov, and without firing a single shot, made their way into the city with no resistance.[239] Russia reported that Ukraine's military and government were so demoralized and discombobulated that they didn't even declare war against Russia.

[237] AFP (24 February 2022) No 'Plans' To Send NATO Troops To Ukraine: Stoltenberg https://www.barrons.com/news/no-plans-to-send-nato-troops-to-ukraine-stoltenberg-01645703707

[238] Sinead Baker (25 February 2022) Ukraine's president says his country had been 'left alone' to defend itself from Russia https://www.businessinsider.com/ukraine-president-says-country-left-alone-defend-from-russia-2022-2?op=1

[239] VonDasmarck (24 February 2022) Russian tanks in the Ukrainian city of Kherson https://www.reddit.com/r/CombatFootage/comments/t09qtg/russian_tanks_in_the_ukrainian_city_of_kherson/

At the end of the first day, missiles targeted cities all over Ukraine, including many in Kiev. Russia destroyed a Biochemical laboratory in Western Ukraine belonging to the US. Though Western media reports this as disinformation to this day, the State Department admitted in a Congressional investigation, that the DoD has "Biological research facilities" in Ukraine, and "they are concerned that Putin may get his hands on them."[240] Another airstrike targeted the North Crimean Canal, which was constructed and ceased water flow into Crimea when Putin annexed it in 2014.

Water began flowing freely into Northern Crimea for the first time in eight years. In all, seventy-four military infrastructure facilities, including 11 airfields, were taken out of commission. Multiple battles occurred between the Ukrainian military and the LPR People's Militia in Starobilsk, about eighty km from Luhansk.

After the first day of bombings, Vladimir Putin was ready to negotiate with the leadership of Ukraine on its neutrality status—refusing to become a part of the NATO organization.[241]

---

[240] C-SPAN (8 March 2022) https://www.c-span.org/video/?c5005520/senator-rubio-questions-undersecretary-nuland-biolabs-ukraine

[241] Thomas Kingsley (25 February 2022) Vladimir Putin says Russia ready to negotiate with Ukraine in 'high-level talks' https://www.independent.co.uk/news/world/europe/russia-putin-statement-war-invasion-b2023212.html

Putin also wanted Ukraine to end the deployment of weapons into the Donbass region.

Putin proclaimed:

"We were forced to do this; we were left with no other choice."[242]

During a live stream on Facebook, the Ukrainian Military called on civilians in occupied territories to make Molotov cocktails and throw them at Russian convoys, and to shoot them. Ukraine military eve showed civilians how to make them.[243] One video on YouTube showed a couple trying to through a Molotov cocktail at a tank heading into Ukraine but suffered severe burns when the bottle she threw broke inside the car. [244]

---

[242] Italian Post News (24 February 2022) War in Ukraine, Putin: "Russia forced into these measures" https://www.italianpost.news/war-in-ukraine-putin-russia-forced-into-these-measures/

[243] Ryan Pickrell (25 February 2022) Ukraine urges Kyiv residents to 'make Molotov cocktails' as Russia advances and even shows people how to make them https://www.businessinsider.com/ukraine-kyiv-residents-molotov-cocktails-russia-advances-2022-2?op=1#

[244] Tempest Videos (28 February 2022) Ukrainian civilians throw molotov cocktail at Russian armored vehicle - Invasion of Ukraine footage https://www.youtube.com/watch?v=le561ibbebU

THE FIRST CASUALTY OF WAR IS TRUTH

Since the special military operation began, the CIA started working with Social Media giants such as Twitter, Facebook, and others to coerce the platforms to support Ukraine.[245] Bots were created by the thousands to pop up on people's timelines to support Ukraine and its efforts to defeat Russia.[246]

one such source said:

"We are proactively putting out information on the intelligence we have gathered, what we are seeing, debunking claims that are false, making sure our allies and partners have the right information."[247]

Also,

---

[245] Naomi Nix (24 August 2022) Facebook, Twitter dismantle a U.S. influence campaign about Ukraine https://www.washingtonpost.com/technology/2022/08/24/facebook-twitter-us-influence-campaign-ukraine/

[246] REGINA MIHINDUKULASURIYA (5 September 2022) 60-80% of Twitter accounts posting on Russia-Ukraine war bots, 90% 'pro Ukraine', finds new study https://theprint.in/tech/60-80-of-twitter-accounts-posting-on-russia-ukraine-war-bots-90-pro-ukraine-finds-new-study/1114878/

[247] Nandita Bose (4 March 2022) Analysis: How the Biden White House is fighting Russian disinformation https://www.reuters.com/world/how-biden-white-house-is-fighting-russian-disinformation-2022-03-04/

"The idea is to counter Russia's narratives and make people understand that things being pushed to them is disinformation."[248]

Any pro-Russian or even anti-Ukrainian reports, whether true or not, were dismissed as sources of "Russian Disinformation." Any time credible information about the Donbass and the attack by Ukrainian Forces on Luhansk and Donetsk that were reported, bots and other supporters claimed it was all lies. Even well-documented information and eye-witness claims were said to be 100% Russian Disinformation. Biden and members of NATO would continue to echo that "Russia invaded Ukraine unprovoked."[249]

Almost all news media from the West reported that Russia was losing, and Ukraine was winning. After Russia's first setback, early in the war, that was true, however they later regained territory in the East and the US continued to echo that Ukraine

---

[248] Reuters (22 February 2022) Analysis: How the Biden White House is fighting Russian disinformation https://www.reuters.com/world/how-biden-white-house-is-fighting-russian-disinformation-2022-03-04/

[249] US Department of Defense (15 June 2022) Joint Statement by the United States Department of Defense, the Ministry of Defence of the Federal Republic of Germany, and the Ministry of Defence of the United Kingdom https://www.defense.gov/News/Releases/Release/Article/3064556/joint-statement-by-the-united-states-department-of-defense-the-ministry-of-defe/

was winning, though it wasn't.[250] [251] [252] Western media claimed that new Russian recruits were being thrown into the front lines without any training. In only one case, a Russian recruite said,

"We go away for a month, twice a year, and practice firing, but we don't train for ambushes. Artillery isn't supposed to be ambushed."

He claimed in another statement:

"There was a soldier in our company who didn't know how a machine gun works. So I taught that guy how to disassemble and assemble a machine gun. I wouldn't want to be next to him in battle. How can you fight like that?" [253]

Western media was also reporting that Belarus could soon join Russia in Ukraine, was revealed as fake news.[254]

---

[250] Becky Sullivan, Laurel Wamsley (19 May 2022) Mariupol has fallen to Russia. Here's what that means for Ukraine https://www.npr.org/2022/05/18/1099885151/mariupol-falls-ukraine-russia-what-it-means

[251] Joshua Zitser (21 May 2022) Putin is losing his grip on power and top Russian security officials think the Ukraine war is 'lost,' expert says https://www.businessinsider.com/russian-officials-thinks-ukraine-war-lost-putin-losing-power-expert-2022-5?op=1

[252] Charles Lipson (23 May 2022) Is Ukraine going to win? https://www.spectator.com.au/2022/05/is-ukraine-going-to-win/

[253] Isabel Van Brugen (21 July 2022) 'No Training'—Russia Recruits Say They're Being Rushed to Ukraine Frontline https://www.newsweek.com/no-training-russia-recruits-rushed-ukraine-frontline-war-1726664

[254] Natasha Bertrand, Vasco Cotovio, Jennifer Hansler and Jim Sciutto, CNN Belarusian military could 'soon' join war in Ukraine, US and NATO

US Media entered Kiev weeks later, reporting that there was intense fighting in Kiev. One civilian with his camera phone posted on Telegram his video of the reporter crouching in fear while standing beside a crowd of patrons leaving a coffee shop, strolling past him calmly and normally. The Ukrainian citizen called him out during his live broadcast shouting, "There is no fighting going on here!"

Throughout the entire war, some citizens in the United States would question if there was a war going on because of their distrust of national and international media. Volunteers going overseas to fight on the side of Ukraine posted videos claiming there was no war in Ukraine. This led to more and more conspiracies circulating throughout social media platforms everywhere.

Zelensky helped to perpetuate embarrasement for Western media by making videos while standing in front of a green screen, claiming he was in the center of Kiev. Many memes came

---

officials say https://edition.cnn.com/2022/03/22/europe/belarus-ukraine/index.html

out with Zelensky behind humourous background images, as everyone could tell the video was fake.

On February 24th, Russian forces gained control of Snake Island, a Ukrainian territory in the Black Sea near Odessa.

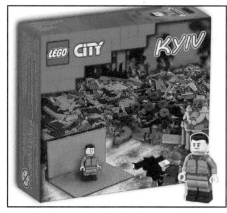

Figure 28: Fake Lego Zelensky in Kiev package--Courtesy Culture War Room

Figure 27: Telegram pokes fun at Zelensky's green screen commentaries--Courtesy Operation Z

Western media reported that all eighty-two Ukrainian soldiers stationed there were executed by Russian forces. [255] However, the following day, the Ukrainian soldiers were seen surrendering as prisoners of war on the docks near Sevastopol. They were disarmed and eventually returned to their homes and

---

[255] BBC (25 February 2022) Snake Island: Ukraine says soldiers killed after refusing to surrender https://www.bbc.com/news/world-europe-60522454

families,[256] proving once again, the real disinformation came prodominently from Ukaine, and Western news media.

In March 2022, Russian Special Forces alleged that they found numerous documents signed by US Pentagon officials utilizing biological laboratories for the purpose of Biological Weapons research and manufacturing in Ukraine and Georgia. White House press Jen Psaki reported that Russia's claims of biological weapons labs and Chemical Weapons labs as, "preposterous" and warned of "Disinformation" campaigns.[257]

Days later, a Congressional hearing took place with Undersecretary of State Victoria Nuland, under oath, admitted there were US-funded biochemical laboratories in Ukraine.[258] [259] Though they claim they were for non-biological weapons

---

[256] Sebastian Shukla, Lianne Kolirin (28 February 2022) The defiant soldiers of Snake Island are actually 'alive and well,' says Ukraine's navy https://www.cnn.com/2022/02/28/europe/snake-island-ukraine-russia-survivors-alive-intl/index.html

[257] Mariana Alfaro, Adela Suliman (10 March 2022) White House warns Russia could use chemical weapons in Ukraine, rejects false 'conspiracy' of U.S. biolabs https://www.washingtonpost.com/world/2022/03/10/ukraine-russia-disinformation-us-biolabs-chemical-weapons/

[258] C-SPAN (8 March 2022) https://www.c-span.org/video/?c5005520/senator-rubio-questions-undersecretary-nuland-biolabs-ukraine

[259] Ed Pilkington, Gloria Olapipo (22 March 2022) What are Russia's biological weapons claims and what's actually happening? https://www.theguardian.com/world/2022/mar/11/russia-biological-weapon-claim-us-un-ukraine-bio-labs-explainer

research and development, the list of items ordered to be destroyed by Kiev included Anthrax, among other agents.[260] Nevertheless, all of the mainstream media networks and fact-checking websites still contend, to this day, that Bio labs in Ukraine are a "Right-Wing conspiracy theory."

The Defense Threat Reduction Agency (DTRA), a structure controlled by the US Pentagon, developed a Ukrainian-American program for the study of dangerous biological objects. US military biologists managed to achieve significant success over its 16 years of existence Acting Deputy Joseph Pennington, the project acting director, Ukraine received more than $200 million from the Pentagon to open 15 bio labs across Ukraine. [261] [262]

As Russia made its way into Ukraine, according to the RF, Kiev gave the order for mayors in many principalities to burn any documented evidence of Biochemical Laboratories. US

[260] Judicial Watch (10 November 2022) Judicial Watch: Defense Department Records Reveal U.S. Funding of Anthrax Laboratory Activities in Ukraine https://www.judicialwatch.org/dod-records-anthrax-lab/

[261] Geoff Earle, Harriet Alexander (15 March 2022) The 46 US labs in Ukraine and the $200 Pentagon program that sparked a propaganda war: How ex-Soviet facilities housing pathogens prompted Kremlin claims America is building bioweapons in Putin's back yard https://www.dailymail.co.uk/news/article-10615639/I-said-no-thing-Tulsi-Gabbard-denies-claiming-making-bioweapons-Ukraine-says-Mitt-Romney-RESIGN-doesnt-evidence-claims-treasonous.html

[262] UKR LEAKS_eng (20 November 2022) https://t.me/ukr_leaks_eng/1129

Embassy in Ukraine, likewise, removed documents about bio labs from the official website. Russia aledged scientists on the inside, however, were able to save some official documents and send them to Moscow. [263]

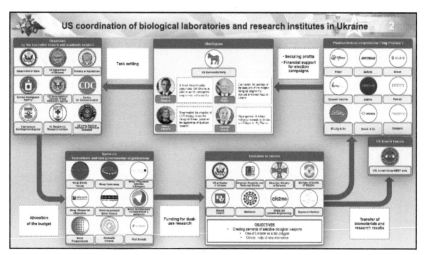

Figure 29: Investigation reveals personnel responsible for US Biolabs—Courtesy Russian Ministry of Defense

Russia compiled a comprehensive chart allegedly tying US personnel to Bio labs in Ukraine and Poland. The first slide shows the cooperation of members of the Obama Administration and various pharmacological companies having ties to the development of biological agents in Ukraine. The

---

[263] Health Cluster, WHO (November 2020) Mariupol City Branch of Donetsk Oblast Laboratory Center of MOH, Laboratory of Especially Dangerous Infections and Laboratory of Virology (GCA) Laboratory Assessment Report
https://reliefweb.int/sites/reliefweb.int/files/resources/laboratory_assess ment_report_mariupol.pdf

second slide shows the documentation authorizing the destruction of multiple agents in the laboratories.[264]

This presentation was deleted from every major website it was posted on. If true, this would be one of the most blatant violations of international law regarding the manufacturing of biological weapons ever devised by the United States.

Another example of Ukrainian disinformation was conducted by the AFU, which was seen on camera, a squad

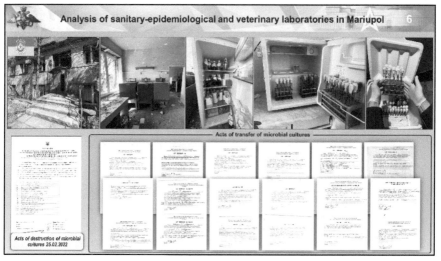

Figure 30: Analysis of laboratories in Mariupol—Courtesy Russian Ministry of Defense

---

[264] Russia Main News (5 December 2022) Russia's Defence Ministry Revealed More Details on Ukraine's Biolabs https://ru-main.ru/russias-defence-ministry-revealed-more-details-on-ukraines-biolabs/

sneaking up to the treeline with their flag, then running low through the field and setting up a Ukrainian flag in front of a territorial sign, just for a propaganda photo-op. This was supposed to show they had captured this particular territory. Seconds later, when their task was completed, they returned to the treeline with their flag, where they had appeared.

A video went viral in November of 2022 of a pregnant woman in Mariupol running away from a hospital, which Western media reported had been shelled by a Russian missile. The world was outraged and demanded Russia be investigated for war crimes. Russian media claimed, a more extended version of the same video of the incident came out, showing injured people being rolled into the hospital on a gurney, not away from the hospital.

Figure 31: Marianna Vyshemirskaya at the scene of the Mariupol maternity hospital strike—Courtesy (AP Photo/Mstyslav Chernov)

The blond woman would also appear again in another viral news video that was reporting on the food crisis in Ukraine. The blonde woman, Mariana Vishegirskaya, a "Beauty Blogger," was interviewed later, admitting that she was pressured into doing an interview because her picture went viral. She claimed the media only published thirty seconds of a video where she said, "There was an explosion," but omitted the part where she stated, "There was no airstrike on the hospital." She claimed it was an explosion inside of the building.

Russia later admitted that they did fire on the building, but it was due to Ukrainian forces taking over the building.[265] This strategy by Ukraine can be verified by the report issued by Amnisty International.[266]

On February 24th, 2024, heavy battles took place in the Sumy region. Snake Island was captured, and the Russian Army was greeted by locals on the road to Ilovaisk. Buk missile systems were rolling through the Kherson region. Law Enforcement agencies of Ukraine reported that Russian DRGs had taken control of the armored vehicles of the National Guard, changed into their uniforms, and took positions in the Ukrainian rear.

It was reported by the Russian Ministry of Defense that Russian Airborne Forces took complete control of the Chernobyl nuclear power plant. President Zelensky tweeted,

"This is a declaration of war against the whole of Europe."[267]

---

[265] Li Cohen (17 May 2022) Marianna Vyshemirsky, pregnant woman whose photo went viral following Mariupol hospital bombing, speaks out about attack's aftermath https://www.cbsnews.com/news/marianna-vyshemirsky-pregnant-woman-mariupol-hospital-bombing-speaks-out/

[266] Amnisty International (4 August 2022) Ukraine: Ukrainian fighting tactics endanger civilians https://www.amnesty.org/en/latest/news/2022/08/ukraine-ukrainian-fighting-tactics-endanger-civilians/

[267] Maria Tsvetkova, Natalia Zinets, Hugh Lawson, Jonathan Oatis (24 February 2022) Chernobyl power plant captured by Russian forces - Ukrainian official https://www.reuters.com/world/europe/chernobyl-power-plant-captured-by-russian-forces-ukrainian-official-2022-02-24/

Zelensky would try many times to get NATO physically involved in the fighting against Russia.

Figure 32: Ukrainian and Russian soldiers sit side by side to monitor Chernobyl—Courtesy RIA NOVOSTI

It was reported by RIA NOVOSTI that an agreement was aledgedly made between the Ukrainian Nuclear Power Plant protection battalion on Russian and Ukrainian "joint security" of the power units at Chernobyl.[268]

Media reports told stories of Russia trying to destroy the power plant, which was obvious disinformation,[269] given that the IAEA would later work closely with Russia and Ukraine to develop a safe zone to protect the Zaporizhzhia NPP from Ukrainian forces attacks on the facility. On October 11th, 2022, the IAEA mensions in its article that it wants to:

[268] RIA NOVOSTI (26 February 2022) Defense Ministry showed video how military men from Russia and Ukraine guard the Chernobyl https://ria.ru/20220226/chaes-1775301254.html

[269] BBC News (25 February 2022) Russian forces seize Chernobyl nuclear power plant https://www.bbc.com/news/world-us-canada-60514228

"implement such a protection zone as soon as possible from shelling at or near Europe's largest nuclear power plant."

The IAEA didn't mension that the attacks on the plant were coming from Ukraine; however, it would seem, since Russia had already captured the facility on March 4th, 2022, it would be highly unlikely that Russia fired on the facility it was occupying.

The Russian Federation even expressed concerns about the UN disrupting IAEA staff rotation.[270] Though the safe zone was never established, the IAEA continued to negotiate with Russia and Ukraine as fighting continued around the facility, both accusing the other of damaging the Plant.[271]

[270] Jake Cordell, Guy Faulconbridge (21 February 2023) Russia says concerned by UN disrupting IAEA staff rotation at Zaporizhzhia plant https://www.reuters.com/world/europe/russia-says-concerned-by-un-disrupting-iaea-staff-rotation-zaporizhzhia-plant-2023-02-22/

[271] IAEA (11 October 2022) IAEA's Grossi Meets Russia's Putin to Help Prevent Nuclear Accident in Ukraine, Calls for ZNPP Safety and Security Protection Zone https://www.iaea.org/newscenter/pressreleases/iaeas-grossi-meets-russias-putin-to-help-prevent-nuclear-accident-in-ukraine-calls-for-znpp-safety-and-security-protection-zone

Figure 33: AFU station assets in civilian areas—
Courtesy aoav.org.uk

A British tabloid was showing photos of different Russian military assets and showed the photo above as an example. Reports later revealed that this was more likely the AFU setting up Soviet Era 122-mm D-30 howitzers on a football field between residential apartment buildings in Severodonetsk. [272] A closer look at the photo shows the soldier on the far right had yellow on his arm patch, which is indicative of the Ukrainian flag. Many armies in Eastern Europe use D-30 howitzers, such as Estonia, Germany, the Kurds, and others. Similar photos and videos revealed the Ukrainian military occupying schools and using public buildings to hide tanks and other military vehicles. [273]

---

[272] James Hardy (14 March 2022) What Explosive Weapons are the Russians using in Ukraine? https://aoav.org.uk/2022/russias-arsenal-of-explosive-weapons-in-ukraine/

[273] Amnesty International (4 August 2022) Ukraine: Ukrainian fighting tactics endanger civilians https://www.amnesty.org/en/latest/news/2022/08/ukraine-ukrainian-fighting-tactics-endanger-civilians/

RUSSIA BEGINS CAPTURING TERRITORY

As the battles began, a video was published of Chechnya forces arriving in the Donbass, which was coordinated by Ramzan Kadyrov. This was the first reaveal of Christian and Muslim forces working together to fight in the Special military operation in Ukraine.

Russian Special Forces were given the order to commandeer a flight of the former Prime Minister Turchynov from leaving Ukraine. He was to be tried by Russia for alleged war crimes in the Donbass region.[274]

The Special military operation began with an aggressive and underestimated offensive from Belarus and Western Russia. Troops mobilized into Kursk, Belgorod, Taganrog, and Crimea into the nearby cities in Ukraine. Russia expected to break through enemy lines and make their way into Kiev within days. Even Western military experts estimated Russia would overtake the Ukrainian government within 72 hours.[275] Gunshots were heard throughout the city of Kiev for many days. Russian and

---

[274] Intel Slava Z (25 February 2022) https://t.me/intelslava/20482

[275] Jacqui Heinrich, Adam Sabes (5 February 2022) Gen. Milley says Kyiv could fall within 72 hours if Russia decides to invade Ukraine. https://www.foxnews.com/us/gen-milley-says-kyiv-could-fall-within-72-hours-if-russia-decides-to-invade-ukraine-sources

Peoples Republic forces had taken control and were battling with Ukrainian forces as far west as Volnovakha.

From February 24th, 2022, Russia began gaining territory in Northern and Eastern Ukraine at a phenomenal rate. Russia had already taken possession of the region between Chernobyl and Ivankiv and funneled their way to the capital. Troops in Crimea made their offensive Northward into Kherson, Nova Kakhovka,

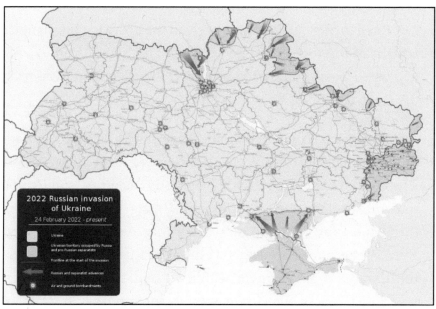

Figure 34: Map of Russian invasion entry points—Courtesy Wikimedia Commons

and Melitopol. Video from witnesses observed Russian helicopters striking Azov troops in Poltava.

The Gostomel airfield in the suburbs of Kiev was captured by Russian soldiers while eliminating more than two hundred nationalists from the special units of Ukraine.[276]Russian Bear Net was activated, indicating Strategic Bombers were on the way. The Russian Air Force Ilyushin Il-96 RSD004 became air-born from Havana, Cuba.[277] DPR fighters began replacing Ukrainian flags with those of the DPR in Nikolaevka.

The Russian offensive was alarmingly effective. A report of Unknown militias stormed the Verkhovna Rada and government quarter in Kiev. They were reported to be Anti-Fascist security forces accompanied by Russian Special Forces. Ukrainian military in Starobilsk was on the run—abandoning their weapons, while twenty Ukrainian fighters surrendered in Bugas. Civilians picked up arms, as ordered by Kiev. Reports of some looting and robbing of local stores in cities, including Kharkov.[278]

On February 26th, 2022, as clashes between Ukrainian Military and Russian Forces approached the Ukrainian Capital, video footage of even more mechanized and military equipment of the Russian Armed Forces were spotted moving from Belarusian territory into the Northern areas of Ukraine on

[276] Wikipedia (24 February 2022) Battle of Antonov Airport
https://en.wikipedia.org/wiki/Battle_of_Antonov_Airport

[277] Bellum Acta – Intel, FlightRadar24 (24 February 2022)
https://t.me/BellumActaNews/71654

[278] Sierra Marlee (3 March 2022) 'We need this': Ukraine reportedly dealing with looters in a VERY unconventional and humiliating way
https://www.bizpacreview.com/2022/03/03/ukraine-reportedly-dealing-with-looters-in-a-very-unconventional-and-humiliating-way-1208125/

flatbed trucks.[279] Russian troops were expected to head into the middle of Kiev the next day.

A Russian convoy measuring 3.5 miles long, was stopped 40 miles away from Kiev in Brovary, with the aim of surrounding the capital and placing it under siege. The offensive was stalled for several days, waiting for more reinforcements to arrive, and making little progress toward the gates of Kiev.[280] On March 11th, 2022, the convoy was attacked by Ukrainian forces in the rear of the convoy, 4 km from the gates of Kiev. The Russia Federation had severe losses of personnel and equipment.[281]

The Russian Defense Ministry reported that the AFU sabotaging the convoy was destroyed that day. Fighting continued into January but met with heavy resistance from Ukrainian Forces. Advancement into Kiev was not possible. Most of Ukraine's troops were defending Kiev from Russian

---

[279] CNN (24 February 2022) Video shows tanks crossing Ukraine's border from Belarus https://www.cnn.com/videos/world/2022/02/24/ukraine-video-tanks-belarus-border-pleitgen-vpx.cnn

[280] Sabrina Johnson (28 February 2022) Satellite images capture 3.5 mile long Russian convoy heading towards Kyiv https://metro.co.uk/2022/02/28/ukraine-3-5-mile-long-russian-convoy-seen-travelling-towards-kyiv-16186692/

[281] Yaron Steinbuch (10 March 2022) Video shows Russian armored convoy caught in Ukrainian ambush on way to Kyiv https://nypost.com/2022/03/10/russian-armored-convoy-caught-in-ukrainian-ambush-video/

advancement from the north and in Odessa to protect the main shipping port of Ukraine.[282]

A contingency of Russian, Chechen, and anti-fascist forces spent two weeks trying to break through to Kiev, and it appeared the war might last only two or three more months at the most. Ukraine, however, switched gears and, with the help of volunteers, pushed the Armed forces of the RF surrounding the eastern region of Kiev and the northeasterly region back to Belarus. By April 2nd, All Russian forces that surrounded Kiev from the north had all been moved back. Russia retreated.[283]

Civilians greeted Russian Soldiers in Kurgan while others told them to leave. In Luganskaya, LPR forces removed the Ukrainian flag and raised the flag of the LPR. There was shooting reported in Bogdan Khmelnitsky, but it was difficult to report who was doing the shooting since there were so many firearms handed out around the city of Kiev.[284]

---

[282] NPR (28 February 2022) Russia Meets A Strong Resistance https://www.npr.org/2022/02/28/1083603269/russia-meets-a-strong-resistance

[283] Paul d. Shinkman (29 March 2022) Russia Begins Retreat from Kyiv in 'Major Strategy Shift': U.S. General https://www.usnews.com/news/world-report/articles/2022-03-29/russia-begins-retreat-from-kyiv-in-major-strategy-shift-u-s-general

[284] Newsofehrmedia (26 February 2022) https://t.me/newsofehrmedia/5391

The Pechenezh reservoir dam was blown up by the AFU in Kharkov to slow down the advancement of the Russian Armed Forces. Ukrainian troops held most of the Kharkov territory from the south. RF Forces were able to move to Kharkov from the north, occupying the entire northeast region from Konotop all the way to the Luhansk Oblast. That too, would be lost 4 days into the invasion.[285]

Mariupol was being surrounded. Russian forces were taking towns and villages near Volnovakha. Russian military columns appeared near Osipensko village. They surrounded Kharkov, and they overtook Kherson several kilometers west. By March 24th, 2022, Russia had advanced quickly—taking over several hundred Kilometers of northeastern and southeastern Ukraine.

By April 9th, all the Russian forces that were in the northeastern region to Kharkov had all retreated in order to focus on the easterly regions of Ukraine. By the first half of September 2022, Russia had lost all of the northern territories of Ukraine, from Bucha to Terny. By November 14th, 2022, Russia lost significant territorial gains north of the Dnipro River, including Kherson.[286]

---

[285] Sky News (28 February 2022) Ukraine claims control of key city Kharkiv after fierce clashes with Russian forces https://news.sky.com/story/ukraine-invasion-heavy-fighting-in-key-city-of-kharkiv-after-gas-pipeline-hit-by-russian-forces-12552959

[286] Washington Post (21 November 2022) WP: What Russia has gained and lost so far in Ukraine, visualized

Months later there have been many battles between Russian forces and the AFU. Still, most of the territory procured by Russia has not changed significantly, even after the appointment of General Valery Gerasimov, aka "General Armageddon." The world was amazed to see Ukraine fend off their Russian invaders, but the celebration would be short-lived as time would show, the war was going to drag out much longer, and with winter again approaching, Ukraine would have a much more difficult time when the ice would freeze.

Russia's Wagner Group, would spear-head the attack on Ukraine, winning city by city. Ukraine casualties became devastating to the point where they had to abduct citizens from the streets to force them into the military.[287]

The battles were extensive, certainly too many to document in one book, and the casualties on both sides—heart-breaking.

---

https://ukrainetoday.org/2022/11/22/wp-what-russia-has-gained-and-lost-so-far-in-ukraine-visualized/

[287] Lorenzo Tondo (9 March 2022) Ukraine urged to take 'humane' approach as men try to flee war https://www.theguardian.com/global-development/2022/mar/09/ukraine-urged-to-take-humane-approach-as-men-try-to-flee-war

CHAPTER SEVEN

THE WEST REACTS

Crippling sanctions, with the full support of the West, were intended to collapse the economy of Russia and put an abrupt end to Putin's war machine. NATO, led by the US, would show Russia, in no uncertain terms, that the United States was the Hegemony of the world. Russia, however, showed the world the influence and power of the United States over other countries was crumbling.[288]

---

[288] Aidan Connaughton (23 June 2022) Prevailing view among Americans https://www.pewresearch.org/short-reads/2022/06/23/prevailing-view-among-americans-is-that-u-s-influence-in-the-world-is-weakening-and-chinas-is-growing/ is that U.S. influence in the world is weakening – and China's is growing

UNINTENDED CONSEQUENCES

Britain was the first to announce Sanctions against Russia for the recognition of the LPR and DPR on February 21st, 2022. The UK Cabinet gathered for an emergency meeting and discussed a package of sanctions against Russia. Boris Johnson made a statement following the meeting.

The UK froze assets of the Black Sea Development and Reconstruction Bank, Industrial Savings Bank, Genbank, Bank Rossiya, and Promsvyazbank. French President Macron condemned Russia's decision to recognize the independence of the LPR and DPR and also called for all of Europe to impose sanctions against Russia. [289]

The EU, however, announced it would not impose sanctions against Russia for the recognition of the independent republics, at least not immediately, because it wanted first to see what Moscow would do next.

---

[289] Sophie Morris, Greg Heffer (22 February 2022) Ukraine crisis: Five Russian banks and three oligarchs targeted in UK sanctions on Moscow - but MPs call for more action https://news.sky.com/story/ukraine-crisis-five-russian-banks-and-three-high-net-worth-individuals-targeted-in-uk-sanctions-on-moscow-12548650

The Biden Administration announced it would sign an executive order to impose sanctions on Russia. Canada followed suit.

Valentina Matviyenko, former Governor of Saint Petersburg and Senator, answered the call for sanctions with the prediction:

"New anti-Russian sanction may cause more damage to those who impose them. The Russian Federation is ready to respond to them."[290]

The EU likewise issued "targeted restrictive measures" against twenty-seven "high-profile individuals and entities." They imposed measures against all three hundred thirty-one members of the Russian State Duma and made restrictions on economic relations with the breakaway regions of Donetsk and Luhansk.

The EU also issued a sectoral prohibition on financing the Russian Federation, its government, and the Central Bank of Russia. The assets of Bank Rossiya, Promsvyazbank, and VEB.RF was frozen. Australia also Sanctioned Bank Rossiya, Promsvyazbank, and VEB.RF and others. And the US, EU, Japan, Australia, UK, Canada, New Zealand, and Taiwan all imposed export controls on software, equipment, and technology. Poland

---

[290] Intel Slava Z (22 February 2022) https://t.me/intelslava/19691

withdrew five Russian channels from the register of permitted TV services.

On February 24th, 2022, news agencies began reporting that Mr. Biden would announce sanctions that would:

"impose severe cost on the Russian economy, both immediately and over time,"[291]

The imposition of US sanctions against the company and corporate officers of Nord Stream 2 AG, the company responsible for powering and maintaining Nord Stream 1 and 2. Biden also said that new US sanctions against Russia would also affect the Russian space program.[292]

In an Emergency EU meeting, Hungary apposed the package of sanctions against the Russian Federation, which Brussels had introduced. Prime Minister, Viktor Orbán said Hungary would not block EU sanctions against Russia as long as they posed no risk to Hungary's energy security. Hungary also made clear it did not agree to the invasion of Ukraine and supports the territorial integrity of Ukraine.[293] Hungary claimed

---

[291] Radio Free Europe (24 February 2022) Biden Announces New U.S. Sanctions Hitting Russian Banks, Technology Sector https://www.rferl.org/a/ukraine-invasion-biden-new-sanctions-russia/31721549.html

[292] Jeff Foust, Brian Berger (24 February 2022) Biden: Sanctions will "degrade" Russian space program https://spacenews.com/biden-sanctions-will-degrade-russian-space-program/

[293] Hungary Today (23 February 2022) Hungary Also Votes in Favor of EU Sanctions Against Russia https://hungarytoday.hu/european-union-

it would cost between €15 billion and €18 billion for the modernization necessary to phase out Russian oil. The EU accused Hungary of holding the EU hostage. [294] Serbian President Vučić also said he would not impose sanctions against Russia. [295]

The EU admitted that the extensive package of sanctions they were preparing to impose on Russia would impact the economy and the community itself and lead to the EU incurring "certain costs." [296] Despite these sanctions, the EU would continue doing business with Russia, with imports totaling €171 billion, down from €258 billion in 2021.[297]

Biden acknowledged that sanctions against the Russian Federation would affect the United States but promised to

---

eu-sanctions-hungary-russian-ukrainian-conflict-situation-von-der-leyen-orban-putin/

[294] Jennifer Rankin (16 May 2022) This article is more than 1 year old

Hungary 'holding EU hostage' over sanctions on Russian oil
https://www.theguardian.com/world/2022/may/16/hungary-sanctions-russian-oil-embargo-eu

[295] Ivana Sekularac, Jonathan Oatis (25 February 2022) Serbia will not impose sanctions against Moscow, president says
https://www.reuters.com/world/europe/serbia-will-not-impose-sanctions-against-moscow-president-says-2022-02-25/

[296] Intel Slava Z (21 February 2022) https://t.me/intelslava/19614

[297] Gabriela Baczynska (29 March 2023) Factbox: EU keeps on doing business with Russia despite sanctions
https://www.reuters.com/world/europe/eu-keeps-doing-business-with-russia-despite-sanctions-2023-03-29/

protect the American economy. It turned out that the sanctions against Russia would degrade the US dollar's status as the world's currency.[298]

Russian Ambassador Anatoly Antonov stated that the sanctions imposed on Russia would hurt global markets and US citizens but will not force Russia to reconsider its foreign policy.

On February 27th, 2022, the EU foreign policy chief Josep Borrell announced that the EU would adopt tough new sanctions against Russia, including disconnecting a number of Russian banks from SWIFT.

The Central Bank of the Russian Federation published an official appeal to all of its citizens on sanctions:

"All customer funds on the accounts are saved and available at any time. The Bank of Russia has the necessary resources and tools to maintain financial stability and ensure the operational continuity of the financial sector. Banking services are provided as usual. Cards of all banks in Russia continue to work normally. The transfer of financial messages within the country is provided by the Bank of Russia's own system in any scenario."[299]

---

[298] Tim Hains (11 April 2022) Clint Ehrlich: Joe Biden's Russia Sanctions Tanked the Wrong Economy https://www.realclearpolitics.com/video/2022/04/11/clint_ehrlich_joe_bid ens_russia_sanctions_tanked_the_wrong_economy.html#!

[299] Dearbail Jordan (27 February 2022) Russia central bank urges calm amid cash run fears https://www.bbc.com/news/business-60543994

Sanctions against Russia initially hit global stocks significantly. The US stock markets felt the volatility as American corporations announced they would cease operations in or with Russia. The Ruble fell sharply, as predicted, with news of the severity of sanctions being imposed on Russia, but stocks recovered in a short period of time. [300]

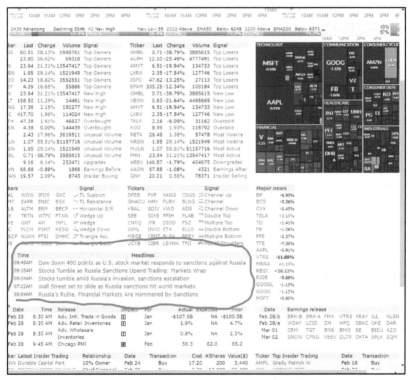

Figure 35: US Stocks head into the red after sanction announcements—Courtesy Yahoo Finance

---

[300] Rachel Martin, Scott Horsley (24 February 2022) Russia's invasion of Ukraine has roiled financial markets around the world https://www.npr.org/2022/02/24/1082766913/russias-invasion-of-ukraine-has-roiled-financial-markets-around-the-world

WESTERN ALLIANCES

Even before events began to escalate in Ukraine, NATO countries, particularly the US provided arms to Ukraine. The US-trained Ukrainian military and Azov militias have received financial aid annually and continues to do so to this day. Since the Special military operation began, the US and NATO provided real-time intelligence and significant financial assistance.[301]

The President of Ukraine held a briefing, where he said:

" If you my dear European leaders, my dear world leaders, leaders of the free world, don't help us today, if you do not strongly help Ukraine, then tomorrow war will knock on your doors."[302]

On February 26th, 2022, the Embassy of Ukraine in Israel made an announcement on social media, indicating the Embassy of Ukraine in Israel was officially recruiting Israeli volunteers to fight against Russia.[303] Ahmed Zakayev, leader of

---

[301] Idrees Ali, Phil Stewart (3 March 2022) U.S. providing intelligence to Ukraine, officials say https://www.reuters.com/article/ukraine-crisis-usa-intelligence-idUSL2N2V62MD

[302] Roman Olearchyk (24 February 2022) Zelensky urges 'leaders of free world' to help Ukraine https://www.ft.com/content/5b423554-6ce9-49fe-b74c-da41298b565f

[303] Shira Hanau (27 February 2022) Ukraine tries recruiting Israelis and other international volunteers to fight the Russian army https://forward.com/fast-forward/483061/ukraine-tries-recruiting-israelis-volunteers-fight-russian-army/

Ichkeria, has offered Zelensky to sign an agreement on military cooperation, which would enable Chechen volunteers from Europe and Ukraine to join forces with the Ukrainian military to fight against Russia. There are more than three hundred thousand Chechens living in Europe.

Syrian businessman Tariq Al-Jasem proclaimed in a video that he formed a militia to fight Russians in Ukraine, but only one of the fighters appeared to have a Type 3 AKS-47. The rest were unarmed. Many such militia groups came out from various states to fight for Ukraine.

Most of the West is a part of, or sides with, NATO, which stands against Russia's invasion of Ukraine; however, there were a surprising number of Russian alliances, as well as EU countries, that disagreed with the call for sanctions.

OTHER RUSSIAN ALLIANCES

The BRICS alliance: Brazil, India, China, and South Africa stuck together in an unyielding fashion. Some of these countries have said they expressed solidarity with Russia and the Independent States in the Donbass. Others wished to remain neutral due to their economic alliances with Russia. The BRICS countries account for 41% of the world's population, with a combined GDP of $26.03 trillion, or 31.5%, compared with the G7 countires having a GDP of 30.7% in 2023.[304]

The countries of OSC: Belarus, Kazakhstan, Tajikistan, Armenia, and Kyrgyzstan, at the very least, expressed their intentions not to take part in Russian sanctions. Countries such as the UAE and Gabonese were against sanctions against Russia.

Azerbaijan and Moldova, in particular, have abandoned anti-Russian restrictions. Even Georgia expressed a desire to remain Neutral with regard to the West's call for sanctions.[305]

In Latin America: Mexico, Argentina, Venezuela, Guatemala, Colombia, Cuba, Nicaragua, and Chile did not want

---

[304] Counter Currents (12 April 2023) BRICS Overtakes G7 In Terms Of GDP, Finds Study https://countercurrents.org/2023/04/brics-overtakes-g7-in-terms-of-gdp-finds-study/

[305] Australian National Review (5 March 2022) List of Countries Not Imposing Economic Sanctions Against Russia https://www.australiannationalreview.com/state-of-affairs/list-of-countries-not-imposing-economic-sanctions-against-russia/

to participate. In the Middle East, Syria, Egypt, Turkey, Iraq, and Iran expressed solidarity with Russia or felt sanctions were not effective under the circumstances. Japan even refused to join the ban on oil imports from Russia until it was pressured to in May. Japan began importing oil again in January 2023.[306]

The Balkan states of Serbia, Bosnia, and Herzegovina did not agree to side with the West, and Hungary, as mentioned, a member of the European Union, disagreed with the original package of sanctions. Hungary also said they would not supply weapons, or soldiers in the anti-Russian effort. They iterated that Hungary would also like to avoid taking refugees, similar to the Yugoslavian refugees in 1990. Hungary also apposed participate in any action regarding gas or oil.

When the EU ambassador demanded Pakistan condemn Russia's action in Ukraine, Imran Khan addressed the nation by saying:

"Did they demand the same from India? Pakistan will keep its national interests and we are not here to serve your, [EU] interests."[307]

---

[306] Sharon Cho, Stephen Stapczynski (27 December 2022) Japan Set to Import First Crude Shipment From Russia Since May https://www.bloomberg.com/news/articles/2022-12-28/japan-set-to-import-first-crude-shipment-from-russia-since-may

[307] IROP (6 March 2022) https://t.me/IR_Pakistan/2928

THE RUBLE BOUNCES BACK

In a move to counter sanctions against Russia, Russian President Vladimir Putin made the announcement on March 23rd, 2022, that all "Unfriendly States" would need to pay their natural gas debts in Rubles, rather than Euros. President Putin said it would continue to supply natural gas in accordance with volumes and prices fixed in previously concluded contracts.[308]

Putin explained that the change would only affect the currency in which the payment is made, which would be changed to Russian rubles. Many EU countries said they would refuse. In order for European countries to pay Russia in rubles, it meant they would have to re-institute usage of the Central Bank of the Russian Federation, which they just boycotted due to sanctions.

President Putin instructed the government, Central Bank and Gazprom to implement measures to switch to ruble payments for gas for unfriendly countries by March 31st, 2022. President Putin explained that "unfriendly countries" must open accounts in Russian banks to pay for oil and natural gas by April 1st, 2022; otherwise, current gas supply contracts would be stopped in those targeted countries.

---

[308] Reuters (23 March 2022) Putin: 'Unfriendly' states to pay for gas in rubles https://www.dw.com/en/putin-unfriendly-states-to-pay-for-russian-gas-in-rubles/a-61234904

The Vatican was the first to transfer ten million Euros to buy rubles from the Central Bank of the Russian Federation in order to make payments. Hungary likewise opened ruble accounts and agreed to pay in rubles. The Ministry of Energy in Austria said it had no way to reduce dependence on Russian gas and would likely follow suit.[309] Armenia and Slovakia both said they agreed to opened Russian bank accounts to make payments in rubles.

The Minister of Economy of Slovakia stated that a ban on oil from Russia would destroy the economy of Europe. During an EU meeting on May 4th, 2022, the talks on the embargo of Russian oil failed, with Slovakia, Hungary, the Czech Republic, and Bulgaria all opposed oil embargoes on Russia. Richard Sulik also explained that an EU embargo on Russian oil would also hurt Ukraine.

The EU developed a plan to buy gas from Russia without violating sanctions and fulfill its obligation to make payments in Rubles. The EU would open bank accounts with Gazprombank and buy Russian gas with Euros, and Gazprombank would fulfill the ruble exchange and payment obligation.[310] It was reported

[309] Infobae (24 March 2022) Austria's industry says there is no alternative to Russian gas in the short term https://www.infobae.com/en/2022/03/24/austrias-industry-says-there-is-no-alternative-to-russian-gas-in-the-short-term/

[310] DW (31 March 2022) Russia says gas payments must be made via ruble accounts https://www.dw.com/en/russia-gas-payments-must-be-made-via-russian-bank-accounts/a-61319393

that twenty European companies had already opened ruble accounts with Gazprombank.

In 2021, Russia exports of Natural gas totalled €50. 6 billion. From the beginning of the special military operation, February 24th, 2022, to May 8, 2023, Russia exported €61.31 billion worth of fossil gas, the top 3 importers were China, Turkey, and India, according to Statista.[311]

Finnish company Gasum refused to pay in rubles, and gas supplies were stopped due to non-payment. Gazprom also stopped all gas supplies from the Danish Orsted and Shell Energy Europe limited to Germany due to non-payment. Shell oil lost between $4 billion and $5 billion in the first three months after leaving Russia.[312]

The Ministry of Finance reported that it was expected to receive one trillion rubles of additional oil and gas revenue for the year.[313]

---

[311] Statista (8 May 2023) Value of fossil fuel exports from Russia from February 24, 2022 to May 8, 2023, by country and type https://www.statista.com/statistics/1306522/key-importers-of-russian-fossil-fuels-since-invasion-of-ukraine/

[312] AP (7 April 2022) Shell says Russia exit has already cost $5 billion https://apnews.com/article/russia-ukraine-business-europe-london-joint-ventures-690e874f6bc51b1c69d1b375a4deb2f8

[313] Barron's, AFP (27 May 2022) Russia Expects $14 Bn In Additional Energy Revenue This Year: Minister https://www.barrons.com/news/russia-expects-14-bn-in-additional-energy-revenue-this-year-minister-01653680407

For the first time, the Ministry of Finance of the Russian Federation fulfilled its obligations in rubles on Eurobonds to foreign holders in the sum of $649.2 million. The payment was also made in Rubles due to the refusal of banks to make exchanges into foreign currency.

One month after Russia received payment in rubles, Vladimir Putin signed a decree of a one-time payment of 10,000 rubles to disabled persons and veterans of the "Great Patriotic War" who resided in the Donbass. Putin also paid 10,000 rubles to families in the Donbass to send kids to school, and 5 million rubles to the families of members of Russia's National guard who died in Ukraine and Syria.[314] Many other payments would also be made to families of Russian soldiers fighting in Ukraine, single mothers, and the elderly.

---

[314] Kevin Liffey,Reuters (6 June 2022) Putin orders $81,500 payment to families of National Guards who die in Ukraine
https://news.yahoo.com/putin-orders-81-500-payment-151750352.html

The Ruble dropped to 54.47 against the US Dollar on June 20th, 2022, but rose from there to 82.02 against the Dollar on April 18th, 2023, just under one year after the war began.[315] Moreover, the market showed that Russia was exporting more oil and received more revenue than it did even before the beginning of the war in Ukraine.[316]

Analysis of the movement of ships and cargo conducted by the Center for Energy and Clean Air Research reported that Russia earned about 58 billion euros from oil,

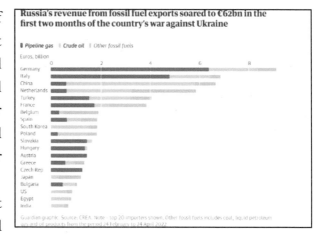

Figure 36: Ruble gains momentum a short time after sanctions are imposed—Courtesy CREA

gas, and coal exports in the first two months of the war in Ukraine.[317]

---

[315] Yahoo Finance (31 May 2023) https://finance.yahoo.com/quote/RUB=X?p=RUB=X&.tsrc=fin-srch

[316] Anna Cooban (10 November 2022) Europe still can't live without this Russian energy export https://www.cnn.com/2022/11/09/energy/russian-lng-imports-europe/index.html

[317] CREA (27 April 2022) Financing Putin's war on Europe: Fossil fuel imports from Russia in the first two months of the invasion

Chinese President Xi Jinping expressed solidarity with Vladimir Putin, saying he respects Moscow's actions. Beijing called on all parties involved to negotiate peace and reminded the United States of who started everything. Xi Jinping also advocated for the protection of Ukraine's sovereignty.[318]

Wang Wenying, the Chinese Foreign Ministry spokesman, said that Beijing does not approve of utilizing sanctions as a means to come to a resolution to conflicts.

"China does not support the use of sanctions to solve problems, and even more so opposes unilateral sanctions that have no basis in international law,"[319]

China called for the United States not to interfere with the legitimate rights and interests of China and others in order to resolve the Ukraine crisis. The Ministry of Foreign Affairs of the Russian Federation likewise stated that Russia would continue to pursue its national interests without regard to Western sanctions or threats.

---

https://energyandcleanair.org/publication/russian-fossil-exports-first-two-months/

[318] Simone McCarthy (16 June 2022) China will support Russia on security, Xi tells Putin in birthday call
https://www.cnn.com/2022/06/15/asia/china-support-russia-security-xi-birthday-putin-intl-hnk/index.html

[319] Global Times, Twitter (26 February 2022)
https://twitter.com/globaltimesnews/status/1497749801684779012

OIL ALLIANCES

When sanctions were being discussed in early February, a reconstitution of oil alliances began to take place. Turkish President Erdoğan suggested that Turkey and Israel should work together to carry Israeli natural gas to Europe, and the two countries would discuss energy cooperation agreements.[320]

Saad Sherida al-Kaab, The Energy Minister of Qatar, stated:

"No one can replace the volume of Russian gas supplies to Europe, it's impossible."[321]

Officials in Austria reported that it is impossible for their country to reject gas from Russia. Martin Wansleben, the head of the Association of Chambers of Commerce and Industry of Germany, also expressed concern saying:

"The imposition of an embargo on Russian gas would be a real disaster for Germany."[322]

---

[320] Tuvan Gumrukcu, Jonbathan Spicer, Susan Fenton (4 February 2022) Erdogan says Turkey, Israel can jointly bring gas to Europe -media https://www.reuters.com/world/middle-east/erdogan-says-turkey-israel-can-jointly-bring-gas-europe-media-2022-02-04/

[321] Middleeastmonitor (23 February 2022) Qatar: No one can replace Russia gas supply to Europe quickly https://www.middleeastmonitor.com/20220223-qatar-no-one-can-replace-russia-gas-supply-to-europe-quickly/

[322] Teller Report (23 April 2022) The head of DIHK: the embargo on Russian gas would be a disaster for Germany https://www.tellerreport.com/business/2022-04-24-the-head-of-dihk—

He also said that Germany has a high dependence on Russian oil, chemicals, steel, and pharmaceuticals. By the end of March 2022, Germany experienced an inflationary shock in the food trade, increasing prices by 6.1% on average, vegetables by fourteen percent, and vegetable oil by seventeen percent and sunflower oil to 100%.[323]

Russia rose to be the third-largest petroleum and liquid fuels producer in the world, in 2022.[324] In 2022, approximately 78% of Russian LNG exports have been sold to countries that have imposed sanctions on Russia. Russian gas exporters: Gazprom and Novatek, have not been sanctions by the West.[325] Canada said it would cease all imports of crude oil from Russia.

Saudi Arabia began negotiations with China to sell some of its oil in Yuan instead of US dollars, similar to how Russia

---

the-embargo-on-russian-gas-would-be-a-disaster-for-germany.rkh6K7fHq.html

[323] Te Local (23 March 2022)
https://www.thelocal.de/20220323/explained-the-grocery-products-in-germany-getting-more-expensive
https://www.thelocal.de/20220323/explained-the-grocery-products-in-germany-getting-more-expensive

[324] EIA (4 March 2022) Crude oil prices rise above $100 per barrel after Russia's further invasion into Ukraine
https://www.eia.gov/todayinenergy/detail.php?id=51498

[325] Center on Global Energy Policy (27 September 2022) Q&A | Why Under-the-Radar Russian LNG Exports Matter
https://www.energypolicy.columbia.edu/publications/qa-why-under-radar-russian-lng-exports-matter/

changed its oil sales. They also said they were unhappy with US security commitments. US authorities are concerned that the role of the Dollar in the world will be weakened due to the new China-Russia-Saudi oil alliance.[326]

Despite Joe Biden's request for OPEC to increase oil production, OPEC refused. The Saudis said they didn't want to harm themselves economically by lowering the cost of raw materials. On several occasions, the Crown Prince refused to take Joe Biden's phone calls.[327]

Russia approached India in mid-March 2022 to ask India to consider buying Russian oil at $60.00 a barrel and other product at a discount, amongst sanctions. India imports 80% of its oil needs from other countries and about 2% to 3% from Russia.

Oil prices have increased by fourty percent during that time, and officials from the Indian government said they would be happy to take Russia up on its offer. India increased oil imports from Russia four times what was purchased previously. Amidst US and NATO pressure to distance itself from Russia,

---

[326] Nadeen Ebrahim (9 December 2022) Saudi Arabia and China will align on everything from security to oil, but agree not to interfere on domestic issues https://www.cnn.com/2022/12/09/middleeast/china-xi-jinping-saudi-arabia-policy-intl/index.html

[327] Bill Bostock (9 March 2022) Saudi crown prince snubbed Biden's request to discuss the oil crisis brought about by Russia's invasion of Ukraine, report says https://www.businessinsider.com/saudi-mbs-rejected-biden-request-discuss-russia-oil-crisis-wsj-2022-3?op=1

India insisted it will not impose sanctions against buying oil and intends to buy even more in the coming months. [328]

It was reported on March 24th that Russia was also accepting Bitcoin Cryptocurrencies as payments for oil and gas. By late April, Russian oil sales exceeded the previous year. Even though the EU, which implemented its 6th package of sanctions, had to exclude a ban on Russian oil because of the deep division between its members.

Biden announced that the US would release one million barrels of oil per day from its national strategic reserve to ease gas prices.[329] China's CNOOC Ltd. Announced it was preparing to exit its operations in Britain, Canada, and the United States for fear of assets being subject to Western sanctions.

To make matters worse for global oil markets, Russia's first set of objectives during the invasion included targeting Ukraine's oil refineries. By April 14th, 2022, all of Ukraine's oil refineries were destroyed.

Despite the sanction imposed by NATO and the EU, they continued to buy Russian oil. NATO and the EU agreed it was

---

[328] Reuters (14 March 2022) Russia may have found a buyer for its cheap oil: India https://www.cnn.com/2022/03/14/energy/india-russia-oil/index.html

[329] PBS (31 March 2022) Biden orders release of 1 million barrels oil a day from strategic reserve to hit brakes on gas prices https://www.pbs.org/newshour/politics/biden-orders-release-of-1-million-barrels-oil-a-day-from-strategic-reserve-to-hit-brakes-on-gas-prices

okay to purchase Russian oil from a third-party state with an existing agreement with Russia, but not directly from Russia. Though the sanctions were implemented to reduce Russia's GDP to hinder or cease the war effort in Ukraine, buying oil indirectly from Russia only nullified the sanctions' intended purpose.

During the operation in Ukraine, Britain imported Russian oil for 220 million pounds, about 1.9 million barrels—independent, citing a new Greenpeace study.[330]

Senior US officials met with Venezuela's President Maduro in an attempt to convince Venezuela to resume oil production for the United States in order to stave off global energy prices. The US claims its intended purpose was to secure the release of Americans incarcerated in Venezuela, but it ended up being a condition of the easing of US sanctions.[331]

---

[330] Victoria Seabrook (27 April 2022) UK has imported £220 million of Russian oil since Ukraine war outbreak, analysis suggests https://news.sky.com/story/uk-has-imported-220-million-of-russian-oil-since-ukraine-war-outbreak-analysis-suggests-12599462

[331] Ryan Dubne, Patricia Garip (9 March 2022) Venezuela Frees Two Americans After Biden Team Visits President Maduro https://www.wsj.com/articles/venezuela-agrees-to-restart-negotiations-with-u-s-backed-opposition-11646756236

CHAPTER EIGHT

UKRAINE'S HUMANITARIAN CRISIS

Though Western media accused Russia of "Crimes Against Humanity, Russia was, by far, one of the largest contributors of humanitarian assistance to the Donbass region of Ukraine, early on. Though you won't find any statistics on how much Russia actually contributed—outside of Russian media outlets, we do know Russia did contribute substantial amounts of aid. [332] [333]

In fact, the Armed forces of Ukraine, and cabinet members of the Zelensky regime stole, misappropriated, and outright denied Ukrainians humanitarian assistance.

---

[332] Telesur (14 March 2022) Russia Increases Delivery of Humanitarian Aid to Ukraine https://www.telesurenglish.net/news/Russia-Increases-Delivery-of-Humanitarian-Aid-to-Ukraine-20220314-0001.html

[333] Apoorvba Kaul (8 March 2022) Russia-Ukraine War: Russia Delivers 430 Tonnes Of Humanitarian Aid To People Of Ukraine https://www.republicworld.com/world-news/russia-ukraine-crisis/russia-ukraine-war-russia-delivers-430-tonnes-of-humanitarian-aid-to-people-of-ukraine-articleshow.html

THE GENEVA CONVENTION IGNORED

Eastern Ukraine has been experiencing a humanitarian crisis since 2014, with the deaths of upwards of 20,000 people, including children. After the Russian special military operation began, Ukrainian civilians experienced a greater crisis, not only from being displaced or a casualty of the war, but also because of the decision-making on the part of Kiev and NATO, which snubbed peace proposals, refusing to take seriously or to adhere to any warnings of President Putin.

The International Committee of the Red Cross played a very important part in sending truckloads of water, repairing infrastructure, and providing generators, as well as medical necessities to Ukrainians. They, on many occasions, have had to remind all forces on the side of Kiev and Moscow of their obligations under international humanitarian law and the laws of war.[334]

In one instance, in March 2023, it was aledged that Ukraine perpetrated strikes on a hospital in Novoaydar, Lugansk Republic. Russia's Human Rights Commissioner, Tatyana Moskalkova, demanded the UN and International Red Cross

---

[334] ICRC (August 2022) Humanitarian crisis in Ukraine and neighbouring countries https://www.icrc.org/en/humanitarian-crisis-ukraine

Committee call on Ukrainian authorities to comply with the Geneva Convention.[335]

When a Prisoner of war is released, they will sign a promise indicating they cannot immediately return to the front line to fight again. However, according to Moskalkova, Kiev continues to send its soldiers returned from captivity to the front line. [336] [337] According to the Geneva Convention, Article 21, when prisoners of war, and sent back to their country, they are bound to honor their parole or promise not to fight.[338]

On April 2022, in an alleged leaked conversation, Kiev informed Britain that it did not intend to comply with the Geneva Convention.[339] Considering the history of Kiev's tactics

---

[335] Tellerreport, RT (29 January 2023) Moskalkova appealed to the UN and the ICRC in connection with the shelling of a hospital in the LPR https://www.tellerreport.com/news/2023-01-29-moskalkova-appealed-to-the-un-and-the-icrc-in-connection-with-the-shelling-of-a-hospital-in-the-lpr.S14VKm0Q2j.html

[336] CBS News (19 May 2023) Ukrainian soldiers held as Russian prisoners of war return to the battlefield: "Now it's personal" https://www.cbsnews.com/news/ukraine-russia-bakhmut-mariupol-prisoners-of-war/

[337] NewsFront (9 February 2023) Kyiv sends AFU militants returned from captivity back to the frontline – Ombudsman Moskalkova https://en.news-front.info/2023/02/09/kyiv-sends-afu-militants-returned-from-captivity-back-to-the-frontline-ombudsman-moskalkova/

[338] United Nations (12 August 1949) Geneva Convention relative to the Treatment of Prisoners of War https://www.ohchr.org/en/instruments-mechanisms/instruments/geneva-convention-relative-treatment-prisoners-war

[339] Top War (6 April 2022) The Ministry of Defense accused Kyiv of non-compliance with the Geneva Convention on prisoners of war

in the war thus far, and the pleading of the ICRC, the OSCE, and Amnisty International for Ukraine to observe the Geneva Convension, it seems this statement has proved credible.

On April 1st, 2022, Zelensky admitted, in a Fox News interview with Brett Baier, that the allegations against the Azov battalion committing war attrocities were true, with the rationalization of "They are who they are." He also explained that they are "one of those many batallions", indicating Azov is not the only one. After the Special Military Operation began, the AFU absorbed the militia into the Ukrainian Military. Zelensky only mentioned that, in one instance, some of the Azov members were punished back in 2014, but not for recent crimes.[340]

On November 18th, 2022, it was reported by Russia's Defense Ministry, and corroborated by many news sources, that more than 10 Russian POWs were executed on video by Ukrainian forces. They had laid down their weapons and surrendered and were shot in their heads while lying on the

---

https://en.topwar.ru/194548-minoborony-obvinilo-kiev-v-nesobljudenii-zhenevskoj-konvencii-v-otnoshenii-voennoplennyh.html

[340] Breaking Points (5 April 2022) Fox News CONFRONTS Zelensky On Ukraine Neo-Nazi Battalion | Breaking Points with Krystal and Saagar https://www.youtube.com/watch?v=yGiNzgxeoNk

ground. But, according to the Russian Defense Ministry, this is not a "tragic exception."[341]

On at least one occasion, in March 2022, a member of the Ukrainian militia used the phone of a Russian soldier killed in action to call his mother to mock him about how he died and sent photos of the deceased to her.[342]

In another instance, a Ukrainian soldier made a video showing several vials of a biochemical agent in a small refrigerator, with the proclamation that he planned to deliver these agents on Russian troops with drones. There were reports of biochemical agents being used on Russian soldiers, causing them to die within minutes.[343]

[341] Aljazeera (18 November 2022) Russia accuses Ukraine of executing more than 10 POWs
https://www.aljazeera.com/news/2022/11/18/russia-accuses-ukraine-of-executing-more-than-10-pows

[342] Intel Slava Z (25 March 2022) https://t.me/intelslava/23566

[343] Intel-Drop (10 February 2023) Video: Ukraine Loads Phosgene Gas onto Drones, Deploys Chemical Weapons Against Russian Soldiers
https://www.theinteldrop.org/2023/02/10/video-ukraine-loads-phosgene-gas-onto-drones-deploys-chemical-weapons-against-russian-soldiers/

HUMANITARIAN AID

On February 23rd, 2022, Denis Pushilin and Leonid Pasechnik, the heads of the DPR and LPR respectively, appealed to Moscow for help. They asked the RF to repel the aggression of the Ukrainian Armed Forces, in order to prevent civilian casualties and a certain humanitarian disaster in the Donbass region. [344] [345] After the Ukrainian Armed Forces targeted civilian electric substations in Donetsk, the head of Donetsk announced the evacuation of women and children, and elderly people from the region, to Russia, where they would be taken care of during the escalation of Ukrainian shelling in the territory.

President Vladimir Putin made a speech where he claimed that Ukraine was a part of Russia before the collapse of the Soviet Union in 1991, and throughout the events in history have been, at least culturally, ethic Russians. He went on to explaine that the purpose of the special military operation wasn't to harm, or target civilians but to "demilitarize and denazify" the country of Ukraine in order to protect ethnic Russians living in Ukraine.

---

[344] BBC News (21 February 2022) The leaders of the DPR and LPR asked Putin to recognize them as states
https://www.bbc.com/russian/news-60465863 (Russian)

[345] AFP (23 February 2022) Kremlin Says Ukraine Rebels Have Asked Russia for 'Help' Against Kyiv
https://www.themoscowtimes.com/2022/02/23/kremlin-says-ukraine-rebels-have-asked-russia-for-help-against-kyiv-a76548

President Putin published an essay on the historic relationship between Russia and Ukraine.[346]

President Putin explained that he didn't annex Crimea. Crimea wanted to be a part of Russia and annexed itself. Now, it is quite possible that this is the case, but the annexation occurred only 2 weeks from the 2014 election that the United States was caught interfering in. From the tactics employed by the people of Crimea to bring about a revolution, to the skill in which the transition of currency was implemented, we can confidently conclude that the Kremlin nudged the referendum of Crimea. You will find that Crimea historically voted for pro-Russian candidates, which is why the numbers were so overwhelming.[347]

The Donbass Republics, however, wanted to be annexed from Ukraine, similar to Crimea, and we can ascertain that Moscow didn't provoke their referendum, because Putin asked Donetsk and Luhansk to wait, and not vote on a referendum in 2014, but they did anyway. That impulsiveness set the stage for the 8-year war before the special military operation.

[346] Vladimir Putin (2021) ON THE HISTORICAL UNITY OF RUSSIANS AND UKRAINIANS https://en.wikisource.org/wiki/On_the_Historical_Unity_of_Russians_and_Ukrainians

[347] Wikimedia Commons (2020) Ukraine Voting https://commons.wikimedia.org/w/index.php?search=ukraine+voting&title=Special:MediaSearch&go=Go&type=image&fileres=%3E1000

Putin announced that Russia would not be purposely targeting civilians, because Russia needs citizens in the Donbass to manage and run their cities after the special military operation has concluded, and that targeting Ukrainian civilians would be counterproductive and would not inspire cooperation or support. But he did warn civilians in Ukraine not to pick up arms against Russian Forces, or they could become legitimate targets.

There have also been many cases of the death of civilians during the bombing of critical infrastructures during the war, but not with the intention of targeting civilians. Instead, they are the unfortunate victims of collateral damage, a term never used by the US State Department, or NATO in this conflict, but one that Human rights organizations have accused Ukraine for repeatedly.

In the first week of the war, Russia captured an incredible amount of territory in a short period of time, moving past residential neighborhoods. This would not have been possible if the RF were targeting civilians.

Russia's first major humanitarian effort was the shelling of a dam that Ukraine had built, which blocked water from the Dnieper entering Crimea for its citizens after its annexation in 2014. On March 31st, 2022, the Armed Forces of the RF announced a "Cease Fire" in order to open a humanitarian corridor for the evacuation of civilians and foreign citizens from

Mariupol to Zaporozhye and Berdyansk. This also included 430 tons of basic necessities and food.[348]

In all, Russia claims to have prepared more than 10,500 tons of humanitarian aid to Ukraine, which included building materials, food, and basic necessities.[349]

The people's militia of the DPR claimed that it would provide a humanitarian corridor to the servicemen of the 53rd Ombr of the Armed Forces of Ukraine under the condition of a voluntary surrender of weapons which they accepted. Ukrainian Servicemen of the 57th brigade also raised a white flag, got in touch, and asked for Russian humanitarian aid.[350]

---

[348] Apoorva Kaul (8 March 2022) Russia-Ukraine War: Russia Delivers 430 Tonnes Of Humanitarian Aid To People Of Ukraine https://www.republicworld.com/world-news/russia-ukraine-crisis/russia-ukraine-war-russia-delivers-430-tonnes-of-humanitarian-aid-to-people-of-ukraine-articleshow.html

[349] TASS News (2 March 2022) More than 10,500 tons of humanitarian aid is prepared for Ukraine — Russian ministry https://tass.com/defense/1415529

[350] TASS News (26 February 2022) Humanitarian corridor established for surrendered Ukrainian forces – DPR https://tass.com/world/1411745

Figure 37: Russia opens humanitarian corridors in many parts of the Donbass--Courtesy DPR

On April 1st, 2022, Fighters of the NM LPR as well as volunteers, brought humanitarian aid to Rubizhne, as well as conducted evacuations. On April 3rd, 2022, the Russian Emergencies Ministry delivered another 665 tons of humanitarian aid to Ukraine and the Donbass. [351] Russian military delivered more than 10 tons of humanitarian aid to residents of Mykolayiv, which included cereals, pasta, canned meat, and fish. There were no stores open anywhere in Mariupol at this time, so it was critical to provide emergency rations to Ukrainians in the Donbass, as soon as possible.

In the month of March, Russian National Center for Defense Management claimed Russian Forces prepared more

---

[351] Mohamed Wadie (3 April 2022) Russia Delivers 665 Tons of Humanitarian Aid to Ukraine & Donbas https://see.news/russia-delivers-665-tons-of-humanitarian-aid-to-ukraine

than 10,500 tons of humanitarian aid in Ukraine and Donbass by the Russian Emergencies Ministry. [352] This included 1000 tons to Luhansk and Donetsk. [353] On April 12th, 2022, Humanitarian aid arrived in Kharkiv and 19 adjacent villages, with another 1000 tons by late April.

Russia also agreed to support the Red Cross in helping displaced people in the Donbass, just before the special operation began.[354] If true, this means the equivielent amount of humanitarian aid came from Russia between February and April of 2022, than aid provided by 35 EU countries during the same time period.[355]

The President of South Ossetia, Anatoly Bibiolov, along with the "Combat Brotherhood, Dmitry Sablin brought

[352] TASS News (2 March 2022) More than 10,500 tons of humanitarian aid is prepared for Ukraine — Russian ministry https://tass.com/defense/1415529

[353] 237Online (19 March 2022) La Russie a envoyé plus de 1.000 tonnes d'aide humanitaire dans le Donbass en un mois https://www.237online.com/la-russie-a-envoye-plus-de-1-000-tonnes-daide-humanitaire-dans-le-donbass-en-un-mois/ (French)

[354] Cristiano Antonino (22 March 2022) The Other Side Of The Fighting In Donbass: UNHCR Will Support The Russian Red Cross For Refugees In Russia https://www.emergency-live.com/news/the-other-side-of-the-fighting-in-donbass-unhcr-will-support-the-russian-red-cross-for-refugees-in-russia/

[355] OCHA (29 December 2022) During martial law Ukraine received 10,500 tonnes of medical humanitarian aid worth UAH 12,850 million: Ministry of Health https://reliefweb.int/report/ukraine/during-martial-law-ukraine-received-10500-tonnes-medical-humanitarian-aid-worth-uah-12850-million-ministry-health

humanitarian aid to a hospital in DPR-controlled Mariupol including insulin and other medicine.

On May 1st, 2022, two trains carrying 4 boxcars of humanitarian aid left the Saratov region to residents in the Donbass. The aid included food, building materials, and medical supplies.[356] On May 5th, Russian Emergencies Ministries sent another fourty tons of humanitarian aid to the residents of the Kharkiv region. [357]

The US provided over one hundred billion in aid, predominantly military aid, and cash, to Kiev in 2022. At the end of April, the US provided roughly $301 million in humanitarian assistance, $53 million of which went to the World Food Program. USAID sent $20,800 to the Red Cross and another $30,000 to the United Nations Food and Agriculture Organization. The largest of which, $100 million, went to help feed refugees fleeing western Ukraine.

For bureaucratic and administrative aid programs, $2.5 million went to the "UN Office for the Coordination of Humanitarian Affairs." $6.8 million to the United Nations

---

[356] War Chapter @warchapter on Twitter (1 May 2022) https://twitter.com/warchapter/status/1520735038056378368

[357] Cristiano Antonino (6 May 2022) Rescuers Of The Ministry Of Emergency Situations Of Russia Help Residents Of Donbass Within A Humanitarian Mission https://www.emergency-live.com/news/rescuers-of-the-ministry-of-emergency-situations-of-russia-help-residents-of-donbass-within-a-humanitarian-mission/

International Children's Emergency Fund, $6.1 million to the International Organization for Migration, $967,280 was sent to the World Health Organization, while only $11.6 million went to support the Donbass region, but only to those that were partners with Kiev.[358]

HUMANITARIAN CORRIDORS

Humanitarian corridors are the agreement of a protected zone which allows civilians caught in the battle zone to have safe passage out of the area, and in some cases to provide Humanitarian aid to those who insist on staying in the area. In Mariupol, on March 31st, 2022, Russians agreed to the release of "Only civilians" through the humanitarian corridor, but soldiers, including the wounded, who would desire to be transported or escorted out of the warzone would need to surrender. [359]

Though Prime Minister Naftali Bennett spoke with both Zelensky and President Putin about allowing more out of the corridor, Putin reiterated that Civilians and wounded civilians

---

[358] Brad Dress (28 April 2022) Here's where US money is flowing in Ukraine https://news.yahoo.com/where-us-money-flowing-ukraine-164303554.html

[359] BBC News (31 March 2022) Ukraine War: Putin demands Mariupol surrender to end shelling https://www.bbc.com/news/world-europe-60926470

were allowed through a UN and Red Cross humanitarian corridor, unless they surrender.

France contributed to the Humanitarian effort by sending military equipment and aid to Ukraine. Zelensky thanked the President of France for the deliveries of large military equipment that contributed to the Ukrainian resistance. France said this aid and humanitarian assistance would increase.

Deputy Prime Minister of Ukraine Irina Vereshchuk announced that he approved of nine humanitarian corridors for April 14th, 2022, for the evacuation of residents, utilizing their own means of transportation, in the cities of Mariupol, Berdynsk, Tokmak, and from Energodar to Zaporozhye.

ZELENSKY REFUSES TO OPEN CORRIDORS

On March 5th, 2022, six corridors were set for civilians to escape the battles in the western Donbass. Three of the six proposed routes led to either Russia or Belarus, from where Russian forces have launched parts of their campaign. Zelensky went back on his word to allow the corridors to take place, citing that Ukrainians shouldn't be evacuating to Russia or Belarus. Zelensky called this propaganda, allowing Ukrainians to evacuate to safety in the country that invaded it. [360] Zelensky prioritized winning the propaganda war over civilian's safety.

Three of the families in Mariupol who came out of hiding when Russian forces arrived, told the troops they had not been informed of any humanitarian corridors because Kiev did not notify anyone.[361] Other civilians that were preparing to leave the battle zone through humanitarian corridors, were told by Ukrainian soldiers that they were not allowed to leave.[362]

From March 2nd, 2022, to June 3rd, 2022, Russia had delivered more than 25,838 tons of Humanitarian aide to Ukraine, according to Colonel General Mikhail Mizintsev.[363] NBC News showed the distribution of Russian Humanitarian aid for thousands at Mariupol.[364]

---

[360] Times of Israel (7 March 2022) Ukraine says Russia making escape impossible after new evacuation corridors offered https://www.timesofisrael.com/us-congress-looks-to-further-cut-russia-from-global-market-as-economic-havoc-deepens/

[361] Oldman God (5 March 2022) Ukrainian Authorities did not notify the people about the Humanitarian Corridor https://www.youtube.com/watch?v=nUArH6omeKw

[362] Intel Slava Z (5 March 2022) https://t.me/intelslava/21606

[363] NJ News, RIA Novosti (3 June 2022) Mizintsev: Russia Has Delivered 25,838 Tons Of Humanitarian Aid To Ukraine Since March 2 https://newsunrolled.com/world/27798.html

[364] NBC News (6 April 2022) Russian humanitarian aid distributed in besieged Mariupol https://www.nbcnews.com/video/russian-humanitarian-aid-distributed-in-besieged-mariupol-137117765548

BLOCKED HUMANITARIAN AID

On one occasion Russia rejected the Ukrainian proposals for the establishment of humanitarian corridors on June 14th, 2022. An urgent statement was made by the Head of the Russian Interdepartmental Coordination Headquarters for Humanitarian Response in Ukraine.

Kiev proposed to organize a humanitarian corridor to the territory of Lysichansk. This was rejected by Russia due to the destruction of bridges across the Seversky Donets by the Ukrainian Armed Forces. It was also rejected because Kiev wanted to use the corridors to withdraw military troops from the region, which was encircled by Russia.[365]

Mayor Anatoly Stepanets of Volchansk, in the Kharkiv region, it was aledged, had previously prevented local residents from receiving humanitarian aid from the Russian military and was arrested by RF Forces. Many parts of the region were without electricity or water. [366] Servicemen of the Central Military District of the Russian Federation delivered humanitarian aid to the liberated settlement of the Luhansk People's Republic, where only 15 families still reside. The rest of

---

[365] Nina Mischenko (14 June 2022) https://vk.com/wall-112108541_1096873?lang=en

[366] Русская община патриотов Z. За суверенитет, VK (5 April 2022) https://vk.com/wall-145220539_15143?lang=en

the houses were alegidly looted and burned by the Armed Forces of Ukraine early on in the war. Looting was aledged, due reports that Ukrainian forces did not have the appropriate provisions at the time. However, the civilian population had also raised complains about the Ukrainian military taking away their personal transport—cars, motorcycles, and bicycles, furs, gold, and other property. [367]

In other cases, it was reported that aid wasn't being fulfilled by Ukraine to those they agreed to provide for. According to TASS News, Kharkiv was in such a dire humanitarian crisis. Russia had to ask the OSCE and the UN to pressure Kiev to fulfill its humanitarian obligations there.[368]

---

[367] UKR Leaks (12 April 2022) https://t.me/ukr_leaks_eng/114

[368] TASS News (30 March 2022) Russia calls on UN, OSCE to compel Kiev to abide by humanitarian commitments in Kharkov https://tass.com/defense/1430009

Figure 38: Mariupol warehouse stockpile of humanitarian aid--Courtesy Intel Slava Z

It was also aledged that Ukrainian militants stoled humanitarian aid intended for civilians and stockpiled it. Though these reports could not be confirmed outside of Russian channels, it did fit the pattern of corruption the AFU, with reports that were verified. A video later released in Mariupol showed part of a warehouse full of boxes of clothes, pallets of food, baby carriages, backpacks, and other humanitarian aid.[369]

Russian Telegram channels reported that the Romanian branch of the red cross stopped humanitarian aid on April 14th, 2022, to the Odessa region. The reason given was that supplies of food and medicine were being stolen by high-ranking officials of the military administration, ordered by the governor and his entourage. The allegations of aid being stopped were denied by Romania and said they would continue to work with the Red Cross to distribut aid to those areas. They claimed that stories in Telegram about aid being stolen was "Russian

[369] Intel Slava Z (3 June 2022) https://t.me/intelslava/30715

Disinformation" to prevent partners from helping Ukraine, but at the same time contradicted themselves by admitting <u>such reports about devastating level of corruption involving humanitarian aid supplies appear quite regularly.</u> In fact, it was becoming so severe that Ukraine introduced a new law on March 24th, 2022, that toughened accountability for embezzlement of humanitarian aid under martial law.[370]

Massive fraud of humanitarian aid was uncovered, where local authorities found over 10,000 products, such as canned food, cereals, and flour, were apparently being hoarded and sold by stores in Kiev. Kyrylo Tymoshenko, the Deputy head of the office of the President of Ukraine, resigned on January 24th, 2023, due to accusations he took part in a scandle involving food for the Ukrainian Armed Forces. Vyacheslav Shapovalov also resigned following more accusations of fraud. He was responsible for signing off and okaying the food purchases at three times their original cost. Head of the Department of Procurement of the Ukrainian Ministry of Defense Bogdan Khmelnitsky was also dismissed from his post amidst the corruption scandal. In all, 4 Deputy Ministers, and the Governors of Dnipropetrovsk, Zaporizhzhia, Kyiv, Sumy, and

---

[370] ICCRA (18 April 2022) Romanian Red Cross confirming intentions to further provide assistance to Ukraine https://www.iccrp.org/en/romanian-red-cross-confirming-intentions-to-further-provide-assistance-to-ukraine/

Kherson, were dismissed for allegedly taking bribes to buy food at extremely high prices to sell in various cities in Ukraine.[371]

Ned Price, US Department of State, was quoted as stating they welcomed Zelensky's "quick and decisive actions," However, this came just two months after the great FTX cryptocurrency scandal, and collapse, in which Zelensky partnered with FTX to raise over $100 Million for Ukraine right before it went into bankruptcy. A report came out that aledged FTX was laundering Ukraine aid money back to US Congressional campaigns,[372] [373] but several Western news outlets denied any connection with Ukraine aid and money laundering to the Democratic party.

Fact-Checkers claimed the money that was raised for Ukraine was immediately transferred into Euros for the defense effort for Ukraine. However, it was discovered that Ukraine's donations could still have been used in the FTX scandle at the time of the 2022 election. In March 2022, Chobanian, the Kuna.io chief executive, revealed that money donated to

---

[371] James Waterhouse, Phelan Chatterjee (24 January 2023) Top Ukrainian officials quit in anti-corruption drive
https://www.bbc.com/news/world-europe-64383388

[372] Katrie Marriner (13 December 2022) Interactive: Here are the politicians who received money from FTX's Sam Bankman-Fried
https://www.marketwatch.com/story/here-are-the-politicians-who-received-money-from-ftxs-sam-bankman-fried-11670359945

[373] Kit Klarenberg (15 November 2022) FTX partnership with Ukraine is latest chapter in shady Western aid saga
https://thegrayzone.com/2022/11/15/ftx-ukraine-western-aid/

Ukraine does not necessarily have to be sold and transferred immediately. He said:

"Ukraine has not needed to sell the NFTs because currency donations keep flooding in but that the government will sell them if needed."[374]

The sum of $70 million was donated to PACs and campaigns ahead of the 2022 election by Sam Bankman-Fried and fellow company executives. Bankman-Fried himself donated nearly $40 million of that and is listed as the second highest doner behind George Soros. His fellow FTX senior executive, Ryan Salame donated $23 million to mostly Republican candidates and efforts.[375]

It is important to note that the US Senate approved a $39.8 Billion aide package for Ukraine in May of 2022, just ahead of the 2022 elections.[376] Bankman-Fried donated $39.8 million to

---

[374] Nitasha Tiku, Jeremy B. Merrill (3 March 2022) Ukraine asked for donations in crypto. Then things got weird. https://www.washingtonpost.com/technology/2022/03/03/ukraine-cryptocurrency-donations/

[375] Bethany Biron (20 November 2022) FTX founder Sam Bankman-Fried donated $40 million to political campaigns leading into the midterms, leaving some concerned about crypto's place in Washington, report says https://www.businessinsider.com/ftx-sam-bankman-fried-donated-millions-democrats-report-2022-11?op=1

[376] Kathryn Watson (11 May 2022) House approves $39.8 billion Ukraine aid bill https://www.cbsnews.com/news/ukraine-aid-bill-house-vote-39-8-billion/

mostly democratic candidates and causes ahead of the election on November 8, 2022. [377] Then on election day, FTX Collapsed.

Officials from the French Customs prevented aid from getting to children of the Donbasss by seizing money collected for Donbass children and detained a number of volunteers from the "Emergency—Children of Donbass" association at the Charles de Gaulle airport. They were held for 10 hours, and the suspects were charged with "supporting terrorism and criminal circles." French Customs claimed they were providing aid to the Russians. The President of the Humanitarian association told reporters:

"I explained to the customs representatives that, firstly, the purpose of our travel is Ukraine, the DPR, and not Russia. And, moreover, we don't violate this declaration because the funds we carried were much less than the limit of €10 thousand above which the prohibitions are applied."[378]

For three months, humanitarian aid to Kherson from the Turkish vessel Ferhanaz was blocked from entering port due to mines laid by the Ukrainian military in the Black Sea. Russian naval forces were able to recover several mines, creating a

---

[377] John Mccrank (8 November 2022) Factbox: How Wall St and billionaires have donated to U.S. elections https://www.reuters.com/world/us/how-wall-st-billionaires-have-donated-us-elections-2022-11-08/

[378] RRN (14 May 2022) The French customs seized money for Donbass children https://rrn.world/the-french-customs-seized-money-for-donbass-children/

corridor for the vessel to dock at the port of Kherson. Ukrainian authorities quickly blamed Russia for mining the black sea, and Western media was quick to come to the defense of Ukraine with expert speculation. It is not illegal to mine the waters near your territory, but States are subject to the principles of effective monitoring and risk control and warning. Ukraine was warning ships accordingly as it mined large parts of the northeastern Black Sea, but 10 of 367 of the mines broke off and floated into shore. According to the Hague Convention, the Ukrainian government should have warned that mines had broken lose during a storm and were floating into shore. This is how Ukraine was exposed as the culprit of mine laying, and not Russia.[379]

RIA Novosti reported on an aledged Ukrainian shelling of a warehouse full of humanitarian aid Natalya Zarya, head of the humanitarian aid center, said a warehouse with thirty-five tons of humanitarian cargo, including food for local residents, was destroyed during the shelling by AFU of Nova Kakhovka. She explained:

"It was very important for the city, since no one receives either pensions or wages. About thirty-five tons remained in the warehouse after the last receipt of humanitarian aid, it was all completely burned down."

[379] Jan D. Walter, Elmas Topcu (2 April 2022) Experts warn Black Sea mines pose serious threat https://www.dw.com/en/experts-warn-black-sea-mines-pose-serious-maritime-threat/a-61334599

Flames from the shelling engulfed a saltpeter warehouse, with toxic smoke engulfing the city. The US was said to be partially to blame for the devastation because Ukrain used American made HIMARS rocket launchers to shell the site.

Over $100 billion US Taxpayer dollars went to Ukraine with little or no accountability for how it was used. Though, like all wars utilizing US dollars, most of it is pocketed by informants, local governments, or used in some way to bribe locals to help in the war effort. Though there are no ties connecting Zelensky embezzling or laundering aid money from the US thus far, it is important to keep in mind that in October 2021, Zelensky was listed as having established a web of offshore companies in 2012, as published in the Pandora Papers. They showed Zelensky and other partners at Kvartal 95, had offshore firms, that were making content for TV stations owned by Ihor Kolomoisky, who was an oligarch accused of a multi-billion-dollar fraud scheme. Weeks before Zelensky won the presidential vote, Zelensky gave his stake in British Virgin Islands-registered, Maltex Multicaptal Corporation to his business partner, Serhiy Shefir, who later became a top presidential aid.[380]

The humanitarian crisis continues, and civilians are caught in the middle. Kiev blamed all civilian casualties on Russian

---

[380] Jack Dutton (24 January 2023) Was Volodymyr Zelensky in the Panama Papers? Offshore Companies Revealed https://www.newsweek.com/zelensky-panama-pandora-papers-offshore-companies-finances-1776124

forces. The unfortunate truth is many civilian casualties occurred by shelling from both sides. As of January 2023, a total of 7,068 civilians have been killed, and another 11,415 injured.[381]

People will always be at the mercy of their governments, for better or worse, and while Humanitarial laws are created, and in selective cases enforced, they are not always followed, or even investigated. Money for Humanitarian aid, likewise, had no real accountability during this time. We can only hope that in the near future, all war crimes will invoke indictment on all sides, and people to look to God for guidance and direction to a more prosperous future.

---

[381] UN (23 January 2023) Ukraine: civilian casualty update 23 January 2023 https://www.ohchr.org/en/news/2023/01/ukraine-civilian-casualty-update-23-january-2023

CHAPTER NINE

PEACE TALKS—TWO WORLDS APART

Peace agreements between Ukraine and Russia never came close due to interference by the West. Putin's security agreements before the war could have prevented war; Putin's peace talks after the first day of the operation could have ended the war, but the West refused to allow it. [382] [383]

---

[382] PBS (28 March 2022) Boris Johnson Pressured Zelenskyy to Ditch Peace Talks With Russia: Ukrainian Paper https://www.pbs.org/newshour/world/ukraines-zelensky-to-offer-neutrality-declaration-to-russia-for-peace-without-delay

[383] Jake Johnson (May 6 2022) Boris Johnson Pressured Zelenskyy to Ditch Peace Talks With Russia: Ukrainian Paper https://www.commondreams.org/news/2022/05/06/boris-johnson-pressured-zelenskyy-ditch-peace-talks-russia-ukrainian-paper

PEACE DENIED

President Putin tried many times to initiate peace. The Kremlin was instrumental in preserving peace in the Donbass as early as 2014. Moscow took part in the Minsk 1 and 2 agreements with the genuine intention of helping the citizens in the Donbass from being a victim of Ukraine's Terrorist Operation that killed between 14,000 to 20,000 people before the invasion began. President Putin explains:

" For eight years, for eight long years, we have done everything possible to resolve the situation by peaceful, political means. All was in vain!"[384]

NATO, a cold war organization of the United States and European countries, was developed after the 2nd World War. This was to prevent the spread of communism in Europe and around the world. Many believed NATO should have been dissolved after the collapse of the Soviet Union in 1991. Instead, it only continued to expand eastward, allegedly installing political leaders against the wishes of the Kremlin and against the agreements made between NATO and the former Soviet Union.

---

[384] Al Jazeera (24 February 2022) 'No other option': Excerpts of Putin's speech declaring war https://www.aljazeera.com/news/2022/2/24/putins-speech-declaring-war-on-ukraine-translated-excerpts

In an expansion similar to that of Germany in 1941, NATO began expanding throughout Eastern Europe, creating alliances, and surrounding Russia—threatening her borders.

THE GOMEL NEGOTIATIONS

Negotiations between the Ukrainian and Russian Delegations were to take place on February 28th, 2022, just five days after the special military operation began. Negotiations were to take place in person at Minsk in Belarus, but Zelensky offered Russia a different location for the negotiation, which the Russian side declined to accept.

The Russian Delegation arrived at the negotiations. Vladimir Medinsky, an assistant to President Putin, said that representatives of Russia would wait for two hours, until 3 pm, for the Ukrainian Delegation to meet in Gomel. Gomel was the location selected initially by Kiev. Zelensky's press secretary told negotiators that Zelensky would now refuse to meet in Gomel.[385]

3 pm came, and the Russian Delegation was about to leave. Zelensky then called Belarusian President Lukashenka and informed them that the Ukrainian Delegation would meet in

---

[385] Sudeshna Singh (27 February 2022) Russia-Ukraine War: Ukrainian Delegation Heads To Belarus For Talks After Moscow's Threat https://www.republicworld.com/world-news/russia-ukraine-crisis/russia-ukraine-war-ukrainian-delegation-heads-to-belarus-for-talks-after-moscows-threat-articleshow.html

Gomel. Medinsky reported that they were awaiting the arrival of the Ukrainian Delegation and did not sleep all night. The arrival time was postponed several times over the course of the day. The Ukraine delegation finally arrived in Gomel at 12:27 the next day. Negotiations actually began shortly before 3pm, by the banks of the Pripyat River, on the border of Ukraine. The exact location was not named at the time for security reasons.[386]

The Ukrainian Delegation included: David Arakhamia, the Head of the Servant of the People faction, Minister of Defense of Ukraine Oleksiy Reznikov, Mykhailo Podolyak, Advisor to the Head of the Office of the President, First Deputy Head of the Ukrainian Delegation to the Trilateral Contact Group Andriy Kostin, Deputy Minister of Foreign Affairs of Ukraine Mykola Tochitsky and People's Deputy Rustem Umerov.

The talks started out with the impression that nothing would be negotiated after one of the Ukrainian negotiators demanded the withdrawal of all Russian troops from the Donbass, and Crimea. The Ukrainian Delegation had their phones on the table connected with NATO representatives, so they could hear every word of the negotiations. Some five hours later, the negotiations were completed with no resolution.

---

[386] Pravda.ru (28 February 2022) Russia and Ukraine sit down for talks in Belarus https://english.pravda.ru/news/world/150499-russia_ukraine_belarus/

Ukrainian head adviser to the office of the President, Podolyak, said they had discussed with Russia about the possibility of holding a second round of talks in the near future. Vladimir Putin expressed that he would be interested in continued negotiations with the representatives of Ukraine.[387]

The Russian delegation aledged that the demands from the Ukrainian side would have allowed the genocide of Russians in the Donbass to continue. Crimea would have to convert its economy and currency back to Ukrainian currency and hold new elections. This was not a realistic request for the Russian Delegation. The Urkainian delegation used the negotiations as propaganda to convince Russia to hand over the Donbass and Crimea.

Reports that US officials were skeptical over Rusia's intentions during the peace talks, calling it:

"Diplomacy at the barrel of a gun, diplomacy at the turret of a tank—that is not real diplomacy. We are ready and willing, just as our Ukrainian partners are, just as our European allies are, to

---

[387] Patrick Reevell, Bill Hutchinson (3 March 2022) 2nd round of talks between Russia and Ukraine end with no cease-fire https://abcnews.go.com/International/2nd-round-talks-russia-ukraine-end-cease-fire/story?id=83226054

engage in real, in substantive, in genuine diplomacy in order to see if we can find a way out of what is a needless, brutal conflict."[388] [389]

A second round of negotiations took place on March 3rd, where it failed to produce a ceasefire but was successful in the agreement to coordinate humanitarian corridors for civilians to escape the conflict.

Russian Foreign Minister Sergei Lavrov said that the Special military operation would continue while talks were "on-going." He went on to explain that any peace agreement must include a point on Ukraine's "demilitarization" and needs to signal that it intends to adopt a "neutral status" and agree to abandon its ambitions of joining NATO. [390]

Lavrov said Russia cannot allow a military infrastructure to remain in Ukraine as a threat to Russia. To that, Zelensky said in

[388] VOA (28 February 2022) Ukraine, Russia Prep for 2nd Round of Talks as Kyiv Demands Cease-Fire https://www.voanews.com/a/russia-faces-diplomatic-economic-pressure-as-ukraine-resists-invasion-/6462659.html

[389] Wikipedia (1945) Surrender of Japan https://en.wikipedia.org/wiki/Surrender_of_Japan

[390] Stefan Wolff, Tetyana Malyarenko (8 March 2022) Ukraine: how negotiations could stop the war and what needs to happen first https://theconversation.com/ukraine-how-negotiations-could-stop-the-war-and-what-needs-to-happen-first-178820

a televised news conference, "You will repay everything you did against Ukraine—in full."[391]

Putin has called Ukrainians and Russians "one people" and said that he is not fighting the people but the "Neo-Nazis." Neo-Nazi elements in Ukrainian society as a whole have been proven countless times. Western media outlets had reported this over several years before the Special military operation began. Western Ukraine was a supporter of Hitler's 3rd Reich during Nazi Germany's conquests in WWII and continues to celebrate Bandera with an annual parade.[392]

Putin said Ukraine had allowed Nazi-like groups to commit "genocide" against Russian-speaking communities in Ukraine. Kiev and the UN, at the time, dismissed the claim as baseless, but in October 2021, five mass graves were discovered in the territory of the Donbass—one of which containing 295 civilians. The UN rationalized the atrocities by claiming out of the 14,200 plus who died since 2014, 6,500 of them were armed groups, however, these militias were fighting to defend themselves from Ukrainian forces. They were plumbers, carpenters, teachers, etc.

---

[391] Christine Theodorou, Patrick Reevell, Bill Hutchinson (3 March 2022) 2nd round of talks between Russia and Ukraine end with no cease-fire https://www.goodmorningamerica.com/news/story/2nd-round-talks-russia-ukraine-end-cease-fire-83226054

[392] Cnaan Liphshiz (4 January 2021) Hundreds march in Ukraine in annual tribute to Nazi collaborator https://www.timesofisrael.com/hundreds-march-in-ukraine-in-annual-tribute-to-nazi-collaborator/

who volunteered for the militia. There were also 3,407 civilians killed and another 7,000 to 9,000 were injured in the 8-year conflict.[393] [394]

The head of the Russian Foreign Ministry noted that Putin did not refuse to meet with Zelensky and acknowledged that he would if the occasion presented itself. Zelensky said that direct talks with President Putin would be the "only way to stop the war."[395] Ukraine's negotiator, Mykhailo Podolyak, said the two sides have agreed to set up "communication and cooperation lines" as soon as possible to facilitate the evacuation of civilians.

On March 7th, 2022, round three of the negotiations took place next to the Polish border in the same undisclosed location. When it was completed, details of the negotiations remained unanswered. However, Mykhailo Podolyak said:

"There were some small positive shifts regarding logistics of humanitarian corridors."[396]

---

[393] BBC (10 December 2022) Russia Ukraine: Putin compares Donbas war zone to genocide https://www.bbc.com/news/world-europe-59599066

[394] Foundation to Battle Injustice (

[395] Kenny Stancil (3 March 2022) Zelenskyy Says Face-to-Face Talks With Putin the 'Only Way to Stop This War' https://www.commondreams.org/news/2022/03/03/zelenskyy-says-face-face-talks-putin-only-way-stop-war

[396] DW (7 March 2022) Ukraine, Russia hold third round of talks https://www.dw.com/en/ukraine-and-russia-hold-third-round-of-talks/a-61039008

Vladimir Medinsky told the press, "Expectations from the talks have failed." and "We hope that we will be able to make a more significant step forward next time."[397]

The March 10th, 2022, talks failed to produce a ceasefire as well. Ukraine suggested that its Western allies, namely the United States, the United Kingdom, Germany, and France, would act as mediators in the negotiations. Russia immediately denied the request sighting their involvement in the conflict. The Russian Foreign Ministry would, again echo those sentaments on March 21, 2023, saying:

"With such approaches, the United States, Great Britain, France and Germany cannot claim to be neutral mediators launching the peace process. They are not interested in resolving the crisis and are doing everything to maximize the confrontation."[398]

In the fourth round of talks on March 14th, 2022, Kiev proposed creating a 'Swedish' version of a demilitarized state in Ukraine, but with its own army. The head of the negotiation team for Russia stated it was being considered during their discussions. The talks, again, produced little results. Lukashenko

---

[397] DW (7 March 2022) Ukraine, Russia hold third round of talks 03/07/2022 March 7, 2022 https://www.dw.com/en/ukraine-and-russia-hold-third-round-of-talks/a-61039008

[398] David Brennan (21 March 2023) Kremlin Says These Countries Can't Be Part of Ukraine Peace Talks https://www.newsweek.com/kremlin-countries-ukraine-peace-talks-nato-america-russia-1789168

proclaimed that if Zelensky didn't sign the Russian treaty soon, he would sign an act of surrender later.[399]

March 21st, 2022, Peace talks continued for a 5th time, and the Kremlin reported that no significant progress was made. Russia said that Kiev is stalling peace talks by suggesting proposals that are unacceptable to Russia. Ukraine accused Russia of setting conditions of surrender and ultimatums.[400]

Kremlin spokesman Dmitry Peskov said that Russia was showing more willingness to work toward an agreement than the negotiators from Ukraine. The suggestion of a meeting between Putin and Zelensky themselves was proposed, but Peskov suggested that there would need to be significant progress in talks in order for a meeting to take place between the two heads of state. [401]

---

[399] Infobae (17 March 2022) Lukashenko: If Zelensky does not sign an agreement with Putin, he will have to surrender https://www.infobae.com/en/2022/03/17/lukashenko-if-zelensky-does-not-sign-an-agreement-with-putin-he-will-have-to-surrender-5/

[400] Reuters (21 March 2022) Kremlin says no significant progress in peace talks with Ukraine https://www.reuters.com/world/europe/kremlin-says-no-significant-progress-peace-talks-with-ukraine-2022-03-21/

[401] Mychael Schnell (21 March 2022) Kremlin: 'No significant progress' in setting Putin, Zelensky meeting https://thehill.com/policy/international/599004-kremlin-no-significant-progress-in-talks-with-ukraine-for-putin-zelensky/

K I E V   R E F U S E S   T O   N E G O T I A T E

On February 18th, 2022 Zelensky refused to negotiatie with the DPR and LPR. Russian Foreign Minister Sergei Lavrov responded:

"Moscow is seriously concerned about ongoing statements from Kiev that they will not negotiate with the DPR and LPR."

Lavrov emphasized that such statements were,

"a direct refusal to comply with the Minsk agreements."[402]

On May 17, 2022, Zelensky, consistent with his charactor decided to end the negotiations with Moscow. An advisor to Kiev said:

"Negotiations with Russia on resolving the conflict have been suspended" and *"Russia is still in its stereotypical mindset."*

He claimed that Russia doesn't realize that the war is,

"no longer going on according to the rules, their plans, and schedule."[403]

---

[402] Intel Slava Z (18 February 2022) https://t.me/intelslava/18907

[403] Tim Lister, Oleksandra Ochman, Katharina Krebs (17 May 2022) Any negotiations with Russia are "suspended" because of Moscow's mindset, Ukrainian official says https://edition.cnn.com/europe/live-

Luiz Inacio Lula de Silva, former President of Brazil said:

" I see the president of Ukraine, speaking on television, being applauded, getting a standing ovation by all the [European] parliamentarians, This guy [Zelensky] is as responsible as Putin for the war."

Lula went on to say,

"Zelenskiy should have yielded to Russian opposition to Ukraine's moves to join Nato and held negotiations with Putin to avoid a conflict."

Lula also reiterated that:

"The United States has a lot of political clout, and Biden could have avoided war, not incited it."

And,

"Biden could have taken a plane to Moscow to talk to Putin. This is the kind of attitude you expect from a leader."[404]

He said Zelensky's focus should be on the negotiation table and

---

news/russia-ukraine-war-news-05-17-22/h_cbae75f33e93b240273310399b4dc2ab

[404] Guardian (4 May 2022) Brazil's ex-president Lula claims Zelenskiy equally to blame for war https://www.theguardian.com/world/2022/may/04/brazil-lula-zelenskiy-blame-war

not on "Speeches in parliaments around the world." He explained that Zelensky was making a spectacle out of war. [405]

In late May 2022, Zelensky made the statement that Ukraine would sit at the negotiating table with Russia after it returned its territories lost since February 24th, 2022, when the war began.[406]

The Kremlin stated that negotiations between Russia and Ukraine are currently frozen by the decision of Kiev. Until they realize the real state of affairs in Kiev, they can not continue.[407]

President Putin was open to communications between Macron and Scholz on the current situation in Ukraine, demonstrating the peaceful life that Ukrainians in Mariupol and other liberated cities in the Donbass have now, due to their efforts. He informed them of Moscow's openness to resume dialogue at any time. Former Russian President and current Deputy Chairman of Russia's Security Council said:

"NATO countries pumping weapons into Ukraine, training troops to use Western equipment, sending in mercenaries and the exercises

---

[405] Tupi Report, Telegram (4 May 2022) https://t.me/tupireport/4313

[406] PBS (25 May 2022) Zelenskyy says Russia must withdraw to pre-war positions before diplomatic talks https://www.pbs.org/newshour/world/zelensky-says-russia-must-withdraw-to-pre-war-positions-before-diplomatic-talks

[407] TASS News (27 May 2022) Zelensky's statements do not reveal whether Kiev realizes real state of affairs — Kremlin https://tass.com/politics/1456817

of Alliance countries near our borders increase the likelihood of a direct and open conflict between NATO and Russia."[408]

Because of the effect of the global economy, many heads of state and media are urging negotiations to continue. This is due to the miscalculation of sanctions against Russia that is, in fact, doing more harm to the global economies of the world rather than to Russia. The Guardian reported,

" But the harm done to the rest of Europe and the outside world is now glaring. The EU should stick to helping Ukraine's war effort and withdraw economic sanctions against Russia. They are self-defeating and senselessly cruel."[409]

Negotiations through the US, EU, and UK are continuing with Ukraine trying to establish a ceasefire with Russia, which included a four-stage plan for solving the conflict. This was proposed earlier by Italy but was rejected by the United States.[410]

---

[408] Reuters (12 May 2022) Russia warns West over risk of conflict with NATO https://www.reuters.com/world/russia-warns-west-over-risk-conflict-with-nato-2022-05-12/

[409] Simon Jenkins (30 may 2022) The EU should forget about sanctions – they're doing more harm than good https://www.theguardian.com/commentisfree/2022/may/30/eu-forget-sanctions-russia-ukraine-food-energy-prices

[410] Natasha Bertrand, Katie Bo Lillis, Barbara Starr, Jeremy Herb (3 June 2022) Western allies meeting regularly to game out potential framework for Ukraine ceasefire as war hits 100th day https://www.cnn.com/2022/06/03/politics/ukraine-100-days-western-allies-regular-meetings-potential-ceasefire/index.html

On June 16th, 2022, Moscow told reporters Russia was ready to negotiate with Ukraine, but if Zelensky refuses, it's his choice. Deputy Foreign Minister of the Russian Federation, Sergei Ryabkov, stated that Russia will not give up its demands and will decide for itself where to put an end to the NVO in Ukraine. Sergey Lavrov stated,

" in late March, Ukraine laid out a negotiating position on paper that was suitable for Russia as a basis for work. However, since mid-April, negotiations with Ukraine have been completely stalled; Kyiv is not responding to [Russian] proposals", Lavrov complained.[411]

According to Lavrov, Russia will be ready to conclude agreements with Ukraine if Kyiv "shows an understanding that they're needed."

In addition, the Russian Minister of Foreign Affairs said that Russia is still firmly convinced that nuclear war should not be started. According to Russian commentators, when the West begins commenting about the need for negotiations, it's to create an operational pause in order for Ukrainian troops to take a break from fighting and give Ukraine the ability to restock on more weapons before they resume fighting. This was certainly the case for the Minsk 2 agreement. Former German Chancellor, Angela Merkel, would admit in December that the Minsk 2

---

[411] Kateryna Tyshchenko (16 June 2022) Lavrov said that Russia was satisfied with Ukraine's negotiating position https://www.pravda.com.ua/eng/news/2022/06/16/7352935/

agreement was created to buy time for Ukrain's arms build-up.[412]

British Prime Minister Boris Johnson told the media,

"dealing with Putin was like a crocodile when it's got your leg in its jaws and said it was vital that the West continues arming Ukraine"[413]

The US was also pulling the strings on whether to accept or deny negotiation stipulations, and thus, the US and UK interference delayed negotiations for months. Belarusian President Alexander Lukashenko urged Kiev to get back to the negotiating table and never threaten Russia, which he explained has yet to use all of its forces in Ukraine.

President Vladimir Putin delivered a speech on July 9th, 2022, about the dangers of delaying peace talks:

"Today we hear that they want to defeat us on the battlefield, well, what can I say, let them try. We have heard many times that the West wants to fight us to the last Ukrainian... this is a tragedy for the Ukrainian people. But it looks like it's all coming to this. However, everyone should know that, by and large, we haven't

---

[412] Peter Schwarz (21 December 2022) Former German Chancellor Merkel admits the Minsk agreement was merely to buy time for Ukraine's arms build-up
https://www.wsws.org/en/articles/2022/12/22/ffci-d22.html

[413] Andrew Macaskill (20 April 2022) UK PM Johnson says Ukraine peace talks are doomed because of "crocodile" Putin
https://www.reuters.com/world/europe/negotiating-with-putin-like-dealing-with-crocodile-uk-pm-johnson-says-2022-04-20/

really started anything yet. At the same time we are not opposed to peaceful negotiations, but those who refuse should know that the further it is the harder it will be to negotiate with us."[414]

A War Crimes Tribunal for Azov fighters suspected of war crimes took place in Mariupol, Donetsk. Vladimir Zelensky said that negotiations between Kiev and Moscow would be impossible if a trial of Ukrainian prisoners of war took place in Mariupol.

It was reported that The PM of the UK, Johnson asked Zelensky to refuse a direct meeting with Putin, which Erdoğan of Turkey suggested. "Ukraine should become an example of resilience for the whole of Europe. Zelensky assured Johnson that there would be no negotiations, and now Ukraine would demand the complete surrender of Russia. This was confirmed by Ukrainian Presidential Office Advisor Podolyak, saying:

" Negotiations with Russia to end the conflict are not fruitful either for Ukraine or Europe, as any interim ceasefire will result in further aggression by Russian Federation."[415]

Ceasefire negotiations were difficult to continue at this time because of territorial, occupation, and other conditions that

---

[414] Kremlin, Moscow (7 July 2022) Meeting with State Duma leaders and party faction heads http://en.kremlin.ru/events/president/news/68836

[415] Anurag Roushan (25 August 2022) Ukraine Says Negotiations, Temporary Truce With Russia Not Beneficial For Entire Europe https://www.republicworld.com/world-news/russia-ukraine-crisis/ukraine-says-negotiations-temporary-truce-with-russia-not-beneficial-for-entire-europe-articleshow.html

killed the aspect of negotiations before they even began. Grain deal negotiations did occur, however, that was to allow Russian and Ukrainian grain to be shipped to the poorer countries that desperately needed it. But, once again, the West intervened after the grain began shipping, and almost no grain went to the poorer countries but instead went to the wealthier Western states.[416]

According to Russian Parliament International Affairs Committee Chairmen, Leonid Slutsky said it was ready to restart negotiations with Ukraine only in the event that Kiev surrenders and begins a reduction of its military size and that Kiev denazifies Ukraine. Russian Parliament International Affairs Committee Chairman Leonid Slutsky.[417]

It was clear at this time that only Europe wanted Ukraine and Russia to sit down at the negotiating table, as they were the most affected by inflation and high energy prices due to their sanctions against Russia. The US and UK said in no uncertain terms that Ukraine will not negotiate with Russia.[418]

---

[416] Reuters (7 September 2022) Putin says wants to restrict destinations for Ukraine's grain exports
https://www.reuters.com/markets/europe/putin-says-wants-restrict-destinations-ukraines-grain-exports-2022-09-07/

[417] TASS (23 September 2022) Talks with Kiev possible only on condition of its complete surrender — Russian MP
https://tass.com/politics/1512551

[418] Jake Johnson (6 May 2022) Boris Johnson Pressured Zelenskyy to Ditch Peace Talks With Russia: Ukrainian Paper

During most of the war, Zelensky has appeared in countless interviews, posed for many magazines, including Vogue and Time Magazine, and even engaged in TikTok Live with viewers. He has made appearances in US Congress and entertained many NATO officials—even creating a "Walk of Fame" showing all the celebrities and heads of state that visited Kiev.

The entertainer-turned-president seemed more interested in his newfound fame than in negating peace with Russia. This is evidenced by the fact that Zelensky spent much more time preparing for photo shoots than in negotiations.[419]

---

https://www.commondreams.org/news/2022/05/06/boris-johnson-pressured-zelenskyy-ditch-peace-talks-russia-ukrainian-paper

[419] Ryan Smith (27 July 2022) Zelenskys' 'Vogue' Photoshoot in War-Torn Ukraine Divides Public https://www.newsweek.com/zelensky-vogue-photoshoot-war-ukraine-divides-public-russia-conflict-annie-leibovitz-1728470

CHAPTER TEN

UKRAINE'S PROVOCATIONS

Western media reported how Ukraine's Zelensky was an inspirational leader and how Vladimir Putin was a villain. Now let's take a look at the other side of the story. Ukraine was reprimanded many times for endangering civilians and war crimes but was never charged. Being invaded does not grant a country a blank check to endanger and murder civilians, which Russia alleges. Nor does it allow you to execute your enemy, but Kiev was never condemned for it.

ICC, SITU ARE SELECTIVELY BIASED

On March 31st, 2016, US news outlet CNN reported about the genocide taking place in Ukraine in a video titled: "Ukraine: Donetsk Citizens Crippled By War." In it, Diana Magnay interviews residents in the city of Donetsk about the difficulties of living their lives under the shelling of Ukrainian forces.

"Their hearts are hardened against a President killing their own people."

The reporter goes on to explain that only two days prior, a 50 year old woman and a 34 year old woman was killed by Ukrainian forces shelling. Diana also reported that,

"...this is a story that repeats itself over and over again in dozens of apartment blocks with civilians being killed by the constant shelling around Donetsk."[420]

Missile strikes in the populated areas of the Donbass by Ukrainian forces are well documented by Russia and Human Rights Watch. Human Rights Watch reported on July 24th, 2014, Ukrainian government forces and pro-government militias had indiscriminately used unguided Grad rockets in populated areas, which violated international humanitarian law, and the

---

[420] CNN (31 March 2016) UKRAINE: DONETSK CITIZENS CRIPPLED BY WAR https://www.youtube.com/watch?v=1fsMqYqHnN0

laws of war and constituted war crimes, those of which were never pursued by the ICC.[421] This pattern of war crimes is the norm for Kiev and continues to this day.

Figure 39: Ukrainian missile strike July 24th, 2014, Donetsk—Courtesy RIA NOVOSTI

On March 14th, 2022, a similar Tochka-U missile by a division of the 19th separate Missile Brigade of the Armed Forces of Ukraine struck the center of Donetsk. 23 people died, and eighteen were injured as a result.

Ukraine immediately denied it and told the media, "There was nothing further to talk about." However, western media published the incident as "Unverified" and "Russia accuses

---

[421] Human Rights Watch (24 July 2014) Ukraine: Unguided Rockets Killing Civilians https://www.hrw.org/news/2014/07/24/ukraine-unguided-rockets-killing-civilians

Ukraine." SITU Research and Human Rights Watch, likewise, failed to investigate the incident.[422]

On March 26th, 2022, Russia published a video of a missile landing in a crowd of civilians waiting to receive humanitarian aid from Russian Forces. This incident took place in Academician Pavlov in Kharkov, where 6 people were killed, and 15 were hospitalized. Unfortunately, most mainstream outlets didn't pick it up, only reports of the incident were reported on Russian accounts on YouTube, Reddit, and Telegram. ICC and SITU didn't investigate this incident either.

Western outlets were looking for any reason to blame Putin for war crimes, but the lack of media coverage indicated they knew it was likely the Ukrainian Azov battalion. Russia rightfully accused Ukraine of the incident and explained that this wasn't a missile but a mortar. There were no Russian troops within the vicinity of where this mortar was shot from, and the target was a line of pro-Russian civilians waiting to get humanitarian aid from a Russian distribution vehicle. [423]

A well-televised incident involving a missile strike that killed fifty civilians, including children and about eighty-seven

---

[422] Lorenzo Tondo (14 March 2022) Russia accuses Kyiv of deadly missile attack on Donetsk
https://www.theguardian.com/world/2022/mar/14/russia-accuses-kyiv-of-deadly-missile-attack-on-donetsk

[423] News Of EHR Media (26 March 2022)
https://t.me/newsofehrmedia/8033

injured, at the Kramatorsk rail station took place on April 8th, 2022. The missile, a 9M79-1 series Tochka-U ballistic missile, had the words "Payback for the children" written on it in Russian. The missile landed on a crowd of people waiting for the train. This drew immediate cries for Putin to be tried for war crimes. Zelensky also blamed Russia for the incident.

The SITU Research and Human Rights Watch analyzed over two hundred videos and photographs of the site. A spatial and temporal analysis was also conducted. In addition,

Figure 40: Tachka-U missile near the Kramatorsk Rail Station—Courtesy Wikimedia Commons

researchers reviewed satellite imagery and possible sites that the Russian Federation had previously occupied. They concluded that Russia carried out the attack, but admitted that the area it was suspected to be launched from <u>had no longer been occupied by the Russian Federation at that time</u>:

"We also reviewed satellite imagery and inspected a former Russian military position near Kunie village in the Kharkivska region, a <u>possible</u> launch location for the attack." [424]

Russian officials found through their research that the strike was carried out from the village of Dobropole, forty-five kilometers southwest of the city. The Kremlin put out the statement:

"All statements made by representatives of the Kiev regime about the alleged "rocket attack" by Russia on April 8th at the railway station in Kramatorsk are a provocation and absolutely do not correspond to reality. The Russian armed forces did not have any firing tasks on April 8th in the city of Kramatorsk and were not planned."[425]

Kiev published photos of the Tochka-U launch vehicle claiming this was the missile system that was used in the attack. However, the photo Kiev used was a system that had taken part

---

[424] SITU (April 2022) Death at the Station Russian Cluster Munition Attack in Kramatorsk https://www.hrw.org/video-photos/interactive/2023/02/21/death-at-the-station/russian-cluster-munition-attack-in-kramatorsk

[425] Olga Voitovych, Nathan Hodge (11 April 2022) Dozens killed in train station missile strike in eastern Ukraine as civilians try to flee Russian onslaught https://www.cnn.com/2022/04/08/europe/kramatorsk-railway-station-strike-intl/index.html

in the Russian-Belarusian exercise "Allied Resolve-2022" in February 2022.

The missiles in the photos published on social media were not Russian but Belarusian. The serial number beginning with "ш915" has never appeared in the Russian army. Many sources on social media also agree it would be absurd for Russia to write a message of vengeance on the side of the missile in their native language, which would immediately implicate Russian Forces as the culprit. Though Western media claims these are only used by Russia, Non-Western media sources from India have show otherwise.[426]

On October 23rd, 2022, video of an alleged devastating attack on civilians in Kherson emerged. The attack claimed the life of one civilian and injured three others. Ukrainian forces planned and organized a failed attempt to assassinate the Chief of the Kherson pre-trial detention center. Authorities urged residents to leave city areas on the right bank of the Dnieper River due to the danger of possible attacks.[427]

Poland reported that a missile landed within its borders on November 16th, 2022, killing two farmers. Advisor to the Head of the Ukrainian President's Office, Podolyak, reported to media

---

[426] Republic World (19 March 2022) WATCH: Ukraine Launches Powerful Tochka-U Missile In Luhansk As The War Enters Day 24 https://www.youtube.com/watch?v=ZtolJhR76gw

[427] Intel Republic (23 October 2022) https://t.me/IntelRepublic/7384

outlets, No matter the origin of the missile, Russia is still to blame for the warhead landing in Poland. Russia was carrying the war to other NATO countries. Intent, means of execution, risks, escalation:

"All this is only Russia, and there can be no other explanation for any incidents with missiles."[428]

Zelensky also proclaimed that this was a Russian attack against NATO and urged NATO to invoke Article 4 of the NATO charter, which would give the go-ahead for other NATO member states to join the war against Russia. An emergency meeting took place at NATO headquarters to discuss what would be done about the attack.

Joe Biden informed the G7 and NATO partners that the missile landing within Poland's borders was likely a Ukrainian air defense warhead.[429] Despite the fact that NATO agreed this was an attack by Ukraine, Zelensky continued to blame Russia

---

[428] The Guardian (16 November 2022) A senior adviser to Ukraine's president said on Wednesday that Russia was to blame for any "incidents with missiles" after its invasion of his country https://www.theguardian.com/world/live/2022/nov/16/russia-ukraine-war-live-news-emergency-g20-meeting-after-russian-made-missiles-land-in-poland?page=with:block-6374bdc08f08dd2276d83fdc

[429] The Guardian (16 November 2022) The US president, Joe Biden, has said the missile was unlikely to have been fired from Russia due to its trajectory https://www.theguardian.com/world/live/2022/nov/16/russia-ukraine-war-live-news-emergency-g20-meeting-after-russian-made-missiles-land-in-poland?page=with:block-6374bdc08f08dd2276d83fdc

for the incident in another attempt to invoke Article 4, then Article 5, the duty to act.

National Security and Defense Council of Ukraine Secretary Danilov proclaimed:

" I have no doubt that it was not our missile or our missile strike,"[430]

German Chancellor Scholz waved any accountability of Kiev's killing of 2 civilians in Poland by telling news outlets:

"But the main message is that Russia bears the ultimate responsibility, because this would not have happened hadn't Russia waged a brutal war of aggression against Ukraine,"[431]

Later that day, President Dada of Poland said it is highly probable that the missile was launched by Ukrainian forces in an attempt to intercept a Russian missile. The UN, NATO, and other states condemned the actions of Zelensky for trying to involve NATO in its war by falsely claiming Russia fired the missile.[432]

---

[430] Joel Gehrke (16 November 2022) Zelensky rejects NATO view that Russia did not fire missile that fell in Poland
https://www.washingtonexaminer.com/policy/defense-national-security/zelensky-rejects-nato-view-russia-poland-missile

[431] Patrick Jackson, Oliver Slow (17 November 2022) Ukraine war: Kyiv not to blame for Poland missile – Zelensky
https://www.bbc.com/news/world-europe-63656664

[432] Charles Harrison (17 November 2022) NATO row breaks out as Zelensky savaged for 'destructive lies' over Poland missile

Figure 41: Ukraine forces attack churches in residential areas in Donetsk--Courtesy AP

December 9th, 2022—A Ukrainian airstrike hit the Donetsk college building setting it on fire. This is one of 13 rockets that struck the city of Donetsk.

December 10th, 2022—Melitopol: Ukrainian forces allegedly hit civilian areas, which killed two civilians and injuring two.

On December 29th, 2022, Ukraine forces shot a missile outside of its borders, this time striking Belarus. An S-300 missile fell on Belarusian territory which was shot down by

---

https://www.express.co.uk/news/world/1697644/NATO-Poland-Missile-Russia-Ukraine-volodymyr-zelensky

Belarus air defenses. Anatoly Glaz, spokesman for the ministry said:

"We demanded that the Ukrainian side conduct a thorough investigation … [and] hold those responsible to account and take comprehensive measures to prevent the recurrence of such incidents in the future."[433]

January 16th, 2023—3 Ukrainian missiles struck the Kalininsky district in Donetsk City. Three civilians had been confirmed injured, and others were feared dead, having been stuck in the rubble.

April 28, 2023—Donetsk Ukrainian rockets kill 7 civilians, including a child when a rocket hit a minibus, catching it on fire. A Russian investigative officer who declined to give his name told reporters that multiple Grad rockets struck a residential area.[434]

---

[433] Aljazeera (29 December 2022) Belarus summons Ukraine envoy over stray air defence missile https://www.aljazeera.com/news/2022/12/29/belarus-summons-ukraine-envoy-over-stray-air-defence-missile

[434] Reuters (28 April 2023) Russia says Ukrainian rocket attack kills seven civilians in Donetsk https://www.reuters.com/world/europe/russia-says-ukrainian-rocket-attack-kills-seven-civilians-donetsk-2023-04-28/

AFU OPERATING FROM, AND BOMBING SCHOOLS

A picture is worth a thousand words, and almost all of the following shown in this section are predominantly discovered by the Russian Federation on deceased Ukrainian soldiers, and other sources, which are available only on Russian Telegram channels. Telegram is one of the last unsensored platforms available today. Does that make it Russian disinformation? You can make that determination for yourself, since most information on this book is only verified by online sources, and not in person, I can asure you that critical thinking, through analysis and verification of different sources will show that the West is more biased, and a purpetraitor of disinformation campaigns than Russia.

No News network is 100% Fake news, and in reading several articles of the same story, we find, in most cases, non-Western sources include logical and likely details that western sources leave out. When you put all of these sources together into a full picture of what these articles are about, then the conclusion becomes clearer, and we also discover that Western disinformation comprises of news stories that don't necessarily lie, but include phrases of opinion, and leave out details that bring about a different conclusion in most cases—the very definition of disinformation.

The most damning verification of these photos come from an article written by Amnesty International on August 4th, 2022.

The article raised concerns that the Ukrainian Forces are utilizing fighting tactics that put civilians in danger. By stationing troops in civilian facilities such as Schools and Hospitals and using such facilities as bases in residential areas,

August 4, 2022

Ukraine: Ukrainian fighting tactics endanger civilians

Figure 42: Amnesty International article cover photo--Courtesy Amnisty International

Ukrainian forces are endangering civilians, the article explained.

On August 7th, 2022, Amnesty International released a statement after the backlash it received from pro-Ukrainian readers, entitled: "Statement on the publication of press release on Ukrainian fighting tactics." In the statement, Amnesty International apologized for the distress and anger about the findings of war crimes and violations committed by the Ukrainian forces. They also doubled down by assuring the public that they would continue documenting their actions. They stated:

"Amnesty International's priority in this and in any conflict is ensuring that civilians are protected; indeed, this was our sole objective when releasing this latest piece of research. While we fully stand by our findings, we regret the pain caused and wish to clarify a few crucial points. In our press release, we documented how in all nineteen of the towns and villages we visited, we found instances where Ukrainian forces had located themselves right next to where civilians were living, thereby potentially putting them at risk from incoming Russian fire."

February 26th, 2022, Videos began emerging of AFU military vehicles hiding next to public buildings and schools.

Figure 44: AFU stationing on school grounds— Courtesy DNR-Pravda.ru

On March 10th, 2022, the headquarters of the Azov battalion commandeered the basement of school number 15 in

Figure 43: Ukrainian APU hiding in a school gym and tank on a playground

Mariupol, in Cheryomushki. Ukrainian forces hiding and preparing in a school were a common occurrence and did so for the purpose of spreading propaganda about Russian airstrikes targeting schools. Ukrainian forces hide munitions and weapons in the school gymnasium. This is a strategy that comes directly from the playbook of the Hamas terrorist organization, which did the same in Lebanon.

The neo-NAZI Azov battalion sleeping, taking photos of themselves resting in a kindergarten classroom for social media, and in the comments:

"There is no more peaceful place for their brothers in Ukraine except for schools and nurseries."[435]

Figure 45: AFU sleeping in classrooms—Courtesy Getty Images

Russian troops commonly find munitions and weaponry in the houses and schools in the Kherson region. Discovered in a local boarding house was a training base for Ukrainian battalions. The school building was used as the barracks and headquarters. AFU equipment and ammunition were found in

---

[435] @Yorlakh on Twitter (17 March 2022) Azov's having"quiet time"
https://twitter.com/Yorlakh/status/1504368141178228742

the gym, which also included Western literature on guerrilla warfare.

A photo here shows munitions left behind in the LPR after Russian troops appeared nearby. Leaving in a hurry, they also left behind a large amount of ammunition. Above, the AFU stores weapons in school, while on the right, Chechen forces of the RF capture an ammunition depot inside a different school.

Figure 46: AFU storing weapons in classrooms—Courtesy yaroslavholovan on

On March 27th, 2022, a photo was taken by American military journalist Patrick Lancaster showing a deceased woman that was found in a school basement in Mariupol where one of the national battalions had previously been located. This widely contested photo shows the woman had been branded with a swastika, but its authenticity was

Figure 47: A deceased woman found in a school basement--Courtesy Patrick Lancaster

questioned by Western media sources specifically because of the journalist who took them.

Patric Lancaster has been reporting on the hardships of pro-Russian Ukrainians in the Donbass since the 2014 coup. Western sources discount Lancaster as a spokesman of Russian disinformation. Though Lancaster might have unknowingly been a victim of reporting disinformation on one occasion, my

There are little kids here! What are you doing?

Figure 48: Locals scolding AFU soldiers for placing landmines in public places. -- Courtesy--No One Is Forgotten on Telegram

observasion of his videos has concluded his work is genuine, and independed. Any disinformation that Lancaster may have reported is no different than CNN quoting disinformation from the State Department.

In this video, the Armed Forces of Ukraine indiscriminately plant land mines in public areas that children and adults commonly occupy. A video was made near boarding school number 2 showing women arguing with Ukrainian soldiers. "There are little kids here! What are you doing?" A woman shouts. The AFU soldier continues to argue with her calling her crazy. Despite the locals' efforts, the AFU continued to plant the mines in public places.[436]

A video appeared on TikTok of a Ukrainian sapper in a protective suit leaving an IED/Molotov Cocktail on a playground.

Figure 49: AUF planting IDE on playground--@kokosik_2016 - TikTok

Additional photos were shared online by Ukrainian forces, proudly showing themselves taking shelter in preschool classrooms in Verkhnetoretskoe. Many of the stories coming out of Western news outlets repeatedly show Russian forces targeting schools and hospitals in the Donbass, but

Figure 50: AFU taking photos while occupying classrooms in Donbass--Courtesy Sindin History Base

---

Figure 51: Soldiers take photos in classrooms—
Courtesy Russian Embassy UK

now we know, it's because attacks from Ukrianian forces come from these facilities, and Kiev continues to allow such practices, which endanger civilians still living in the area. Many of these buildings are not entirely abandoned, some apartment complexes and hospitals are currently occupied by civilians. Despite reports of mass evacuations, civilians still occupy these areas, because of their occupation, health, or other reasons.

A photograph captures Ukrainian forces seen using school buses to move troops through populated areas of the city. This practice could endanger children through mistakenly targeting school buses that were thought to contain AFU soldiers.

Figure 52: AFU using school busses for
transportation in cities--Courtesy Nairalan Forum

Figure 53: AFU attack of colleges— Courtesy Twitter, t.me / NeoficialniyBeZsonoV

Another bombing in Donetsk by AFU artillery killed at least six people and wounded fourteen others. Urkainian forces continue to get away with this because of the blind support of Ukraine from citizens living in Western countries, who are left in the dark about these circumstances. Western media outlets almost never report Ukrainian atrocities, or if they do report on the event, they blame the incident on Russia. An internet search between the dates of April 1st, 2022, to April 1st, 2023, using the phrase, "Ukraine shelling civilians," produces only one result by amnesty international and a dozen results with the words, "Claims Russian-officials." When searching the same in Google News, the first two results were about Russian forces shelling civilians, and the Amnesty International article does not appear in the results.

On August 12th, 2022, a video was published about an interview with an elderly lady in Ukraine, and she explained that Ukrainian forces were endangering residents in the neighborhood by recklessly placing ammunition on the streets and then shelling it to blow it up. This left us at the mercy of luck, she explained.

Figure 54: AFU fighting from classrooms in the Donetsk region—Courtesy @ng_ukraine on Twitter

On August 14th, 2022, a horrific video surfaced showing the aftermath of a neighborhood in the Lininsky district of Donetsk City. A garden of the residence was destroyed, along with their fence. Shrapnel permeated the entire wall of the house, and lying dead in a puddle of blood, an elderly man—an unfortunate victim of the shelling by Ukrainian forces.

Figure 55: Another AFU missile attack of a college in Lugansk—Courtesy Intel Republic

September 14th, 2022—one person was killed, and seven others wounded when Ukrainian forces targeted a college in Perevalsk, Lugansk. US-supplied HIMARS rocket launchers were used on the college, which caused severe damage to the building, as seen in the video released to the media.

On August 29th, 2022, Ukrainian forces shelled civilian areas of Berislay in AFU targets school in the Kherson region.

Figure 56: shelling in Berislav, the school and kindergarten and the employment center were completely destroyed-- Courtesy RIA Novosti

The US made HIMARS directly target a school by the AFU, destroying it.

It was alleged that on March 27th, 2023, the AFU shelled residential areas of Melitopol, in the Zaporozhye region, injuring at least 4 people, as well as a building near the college was destroyed. 46 students were evacuated to safety as the shelling began at 8:15 A.M. fifteen minutes after the beginning of classes.[437]

THE AFU AND PRISONERS OF WAR

On April 7th, 2022, a video emerged of Ukrainian troops rounding up Russian prisoners of war and executing them. The story published by TheTimes.co.uk, which is no longer accessible on their site, showed images of Russian captives being shot in the town of Dmytrivka, seven miles southwest of Bucha.[438]

This would happen again in November of 2022 when ten Russian POWs were executed by their Ukrainian captors. The New York Times also claimed the video documenting the Ukrainian war crimes was verified. Deputy Chairman of the UN Secretary General, Farhan Haq, called for the investigation of allegations of human rights violations and to bring the perpetrators to justice. The US State Department called on Kiev to fulfill its international obligations. Unfortunately, like many

---

[437] Intel Republic (27 March 2023) https://t.me/IntelRepublic/17211

[438] George Grylls (8 April 2022) Footage appears to show Ukrainians killing captives https://web.archive.org/web/20220408041948/https://www.thetimes.co.uk/article/70865c2a-b6b0-11ec-8ba8-f6bf3099f5f6?shareToken=bf2feaf2fb26407d75bc30ed88225ebd

other similar incidences, Ukraine's war crimes were buried and never pursued.[439]

An interview by "The Times" of a Ukrainian woman named Marian, published March 23rd, 2023, said they had a device that looked like the chamber of an oversize revolver.

"Usually, a Russian vehicle comes to pick up the wounded. We wait for it, and then we use this one," Marian added, patting one of the mortar rounds."

In the interview, she also bragged about how it's better to send Russian soldiers home maimed to be a burden to the state and remind people of the cost of invading Ukraine. This story by The Times was also deleted online, realizing that all she had confessed to be a violation of the Geneva Convention—considered war crimes.

BRINGING UKRAINIAN WAR CRIMINALS TO JUSTICE

On May 17th, 2022, an announcement was made by the Russian State Duma, the lower house of the Russian Federation, announcing it intended to ban the exchange of Prisoners of War

---

[439] Malachy Browne, Stephen Hiltner, Chevaz Clarke-Williams, Taylor Turner (20 November 2022) Videos Suggest Captive Russian Soldiers Were Killed at Close Range https://www.nytimes.com/2022/11/20/world/europe/russian-soldiers-shot-ukraine.html

from Ukraine's National Guard Azov Regiment to investigate them for war crimes.

Chairman of the State Duma Vyacheslav Volodin proclaimed:

"Nazi criminals should not be exchanged. These are war criminals, and we must do everything to bring them to justice." [440]

Russian hackers targeted Ukrainian neo-Nazis, mercenaries, and other war criminals in a program called "Project Nemesis," which is a group of established fanatics who tortured our military and civilian citizens in Ukraine. The phone numbers and residential addresses of identified Banderists are made available to the public. There are dozens of Nazi gangs and Ukrainian special forces listed in the project database. [441] [442]

The very first Tribunals were held in Mariupol, Ukraine. These hearings were being held for some eighty events of the Azov battalion Nazis who committed war crimes against civilians and Russian Soldiers. Sentencing for foreign

---

[440] Reuters (17 May 2022) Russian parliament to consider ban on exchanging Ukrainian Azov prisoners
https://www.reuters.com/world/europe/russian-parliament-may-ban-swapping-ukraines-azov-fighters-russian-servicemen-2022-05-17/

[441] Intel Slava Z (30 May 2022) https://t.me/intelslava/30341

[442] Shaun Walker (22 September 2022) Russia trades Azov fighters for Putin ally in biggest prisoner swap of Ukraine war
https://www.theguardian.com/world/2022/sep/22/ukrainian-putin-ally-viktor-medvedchuk-exchanged-for-200-azov-battalion-fighters-zelenskiy-says

infrastructures and mercenaries was also held in the city of Mariupol. More Tribunals were held in Donetsk from June 2022 to the end of August 2022. [443] Zelensky referred to them as "Heroes of the motherland." President Zelensky himself is also wanted for war crimes by the Donbass for his participation in authorizing the killing of civilians since his time in office.

The Czech Republic allied with a tribunal to hold Russian leaders accountable for alleged war crimes. Russian Foreign Ministry spokeswoman Maria Zakharova responded on her official Telegram channel,

"Start with yourselves, Iraq, and the remnants of Libya will appreciate the active repentance of the West. And Serbia, by the way, too. Untouchables. When are you planning to do justice to yourselves?" [444]

The American Services-Members' Protection Act was bill H. R. 4775, which was enacted on August 2nd, 2002. Also known as the Hague Invasion Act, it denies any American servicemen or officials to be tried for crimes by any non-US court for any criminal prosecution. It also prohibits any local, state, or

---

[443] Reuters (10 August 2022) Russian-backed separatist head says Azov trial to begin this summer https://www.reuters.com/world/europe/russian-backed-separatist-head-says-azov-trial-begin-this-summer-2022-08-11/

[444] TASS News (6 November 2022) Russian Foreign Ministry's spokeswoman slams West's tribunal initiative https://tass.com/politics/1532931

government agencies, including courts and law enforcement agencies, from assisting the International Criminal Court (ICC).[445]

The Azovstal Steel plant was the last stronghold in the battle for Mariupol. A large number of Azov/Ukrainian forces barricaded themselves in bomb shelters and tunnel systems built by Russia during the cold war. Here were also found several civilians—children and women, being held as human shields.[446] Western media would report them as human shields, but Humanitarian corridors were refused by Zelensky when Russian forces demanded the Azov battalion release the civilians from the Azovstal steel plant.[447]

A similar situation arose in Severodonetsk's Azot chemical plant. Russian and allied humanitarian corridors in Severodonetsk were completely disrupted by Ukrainian troops. An estimated 1,000 to 1,200 civilians were on the territory of the Azot chemical plant. Only one local civilian was taken to safety, according to the Lugansk People's Republic Militia Chief.

---

[445] Wikipedia (2 August 2022) American Service-Members' Protection Act https://en.wikipedia.org/wiki/American_Service-Members%27_Protection_Act

[446] ABC.Net.au (23 April 2022) Video appears to show women and children sheltering inside Mariupol's Azovstal steelworks as Russian attacks continue https://www.abc.net.au/news/2022-04-24/women-and-children-shelter-in-mariupol-steel-works/101011702

[447] Aljazeera (25 April 2022) Ukraine urges UN to mediate corridor from Mariupol's Azovstal https://www.aljazeera.com/news/2022/4/25/ukraine-russia-un-humanitarian-corridor-mariupol-azovstal

Ukrainian armed forces did not comply with the ceasefire agreements. The Ukrainian troops who sought shelter in the factory again refused to allow the civilians to leave.[448]

This was a very common practice by Ukraine forces during the war. Many reports surfaced showing Russian-backed Chechen soldiers, for example, rescuing children from apartment buildings that were being held against their will by the Ukrainian military. Ukrainian forces prevented many civilians from obtaining humanitarian aid from Russian forces for fear that RF troops would infiltrate the area.[449]

---

[448] Aljazeera (14 June 2022) Russia urges Ukrainian fighters in Severodonetsk to lay down arms https://www.aljazeera.com/news/2022/6/14/russia-calls-on-ukrainian-fighters-in-severodonetsk-to-surrender

[449] Intel Slava Z (7 March 2022) https://t.me/intelslava/22754

CHAPTER ELEVEN

SABATAGE

Increadably tragic events took place during the Russian Special military operation, The Ukrainian attack against the Crimean bridge, and the blowing up of Nord Stream 1 and 2 were just two of the larger tragic events that occurred during the writing of this book, and there will be more.

THE CRIMEA BRIDGE EXPLOSION

At 6:00 am local time, October 8th, 2022, the Kerch Bridge, also known as the Crimea Bridge, was sabotaged by what was concluded to be a bomb transported by a cargo truck. The Investigative Committee of the Russian Federation's preliminary findings found the explosion killed three civilians and disabled the automobile section of the bridge to Crimea.

The incident was caught at three separate Russian security cameras. Because the cargo truck went through a number of checkpoints, including an X-ray, and visual inspection it was

speculated that it might have been detonated by a remote sea vessel carrying explosives. The attack was also suspected to have been detonated by remote from Kiev.

Video footage from the security center showed the truck beginning to ascend to the tower of the bridge at the time of the explosion. Only two of the four traffic lanes of the bridge were disabled. The deck between the three pillars was damaged, and a train carrying oil to the peninsula caught fire when it was passing right beside the

Figure 57: Kerch bridge after the attack-- Courtesy SECURITY AFP

truck as it exploded. 1.3 kilometers of the railway track on the bridge was damaged. [450]

The damage briefly closed the bridge upon further inspection. Ferries were immediately deployed to resume commuting between Russia and Crimea while the inspection was underway. The railway began running oil again within twenty-four hours of the explosion. [451]

Podolyak, an Advisor to Zelensky, almost confessing Ukraine's responsibility for the terrorist attack on the Crimean bridge, wrote on social media:

"Crimea, the bridge, the beginning. Everything illegal must be destroyed, everything stolen must be returned to Ukraine, everything occupied by Russia must be expelled."[452]

Estonian Foreign Minister Urmas Reinsalu congratulated Ukraine's special forces for the attack on the Crimean Bridge, saying:

---

[450] Jill Dougherty, Tim Lister, Amy Woodyatt (10 October 2022) A blast hit a key bridge linking Crimea to Russia. Here's what we know https://www.cnn.com/2022/10/08/europe/crimea-bridge-explainer-russia-ukraine-intl/index.html

[451] Aljazeera (9 October 2022) Traffic resumes on Crimea bridge, probe into blast under way https://www.aljazeera.com/news/2022/10/9/crimea-bridge-resumes-traffic-after-blast

[452] NPR (8 October 2022) A blast hits the bridge to Crimea, a key supply route in Russia's war https://www.npr.org/2022/10/08/1127640378/crimea-bridge-russia-ukraine-war

"Estonia certainly welcomes this (explosion on the Kerch Bridge) and welcomes the Ukrainian special forces, which are probably behind this operation,"[453]

БУДАНОВ Кирилл Алексеевич, 04.01.1986 г.р.

АНДРЕЙЧЕНКО Сергей Владимирович, 30.05.1988 г.р.

ЦЮРКАЛО Михаил Владимирович, 27.02.1975 г.р.,

Figure 58: Accused of the attack of the Kertch bridge--Courtesy TASS News

The Russian Investigative Committee initiated a criminal case against five Russian citizens and three Ukrainian citizens in connection with the attack. One of which, the Main Intelligence Directorate of the Ukraine Ministry of Defense. Zakharova, the Russian Foreign Ministry spokeswoman, said that the reaction of the Kiev regime to the destruction of civilian infrastructure testifies to its terrorist nature.

---

[453] Daria Zubkova (8 October 2022) Estonia Congratulates "Ukrainian Special Services" On Explosion On Kerch Bridge https://ukranews.com/en/news/886852-estonia-congratulates-ukrainian-special-services-on-explosion-on-kerch-bridge

According to the Russian Investigative Committee, the Main intelligence Directorate of the Ministry of Defense of Ukraine, Kyryll Budanov, employees and agents were the perpetrators.[454]

The bomb, which in total weighed 22.77 tons, on twenty-two pallets were camouflaged in rolls with construction polyethylene film. In early August, the cargo was shipped from the port of Odessa to the city of Ruse, Bulgaria, contract No. 02/08/2022, between Translogistic UA LLC in Kiev and Baltex Capital in Ruse.

The DAF truck, registered in Georgia, crossed the Russian border on October 4th, and unloaded a delivery on October 6th. It went through several checkpoints and visual inspections, including an X-ray scan of the cargo. The cargo was loaded by a Russian citizen named Makhir Yusobov, who left for Simforopol, Crimea, immediately after.

---

[454] Snejana Farberov (12 October 2022) Russia arrests 8 in Crimea bridge blast, Ukrainian military official suspected https://nypost.com/2022/10/12/russia-arrests-8-in-crimea-bridge-blast-blames-ukraine/

Sergey Vladimirovich Andreychenko, from Ukraine, purchased a virtual, anonymous phone number from the internet for coordination and was detonated over the Kerch bridge. Five Russian citizens and three citizens from Ukraine and Armenia, who participated in the event, were detained.

Figure 59: President Putin tours the progress of the Kerch bridge repair work --RIA Novosta

President Vladimir Putin himself drove across the Kerch bridge on December 5th to view the progress of the repair.

The reconstruction of the destroyed section of the bridge began almost immediately. The estimate for the bridge section to be reopened was to be as early as March. Construction workers worked tirelessly around the clock and the bridge was fully reopened ahead of schedule on February 23rd, 2023, less than four months after the attack.[455]

NORD STREAM 1 AND 2

Figure 60: Gas leaking from the Baltic pipeline after the September 2022 explosion-- Courtesy AP

On September 26th, 2022, local time, Germany reported a drop in gas pressure in both Nord Stream gas pipelines that supplied gas from Russia to Germany. The Danish and Swedish prime ministers reported that the assessment by authories

---

[455] Moscow Times (23 February 2023) Russia Fully Reopens Crimea Bridge to Cars on Eve of Anniversary https://www.themoscowtimes.com/2023/02/23/russia-fully-reopens-crimea-bridge-to-cars-on-eve-of-anniversary-a80319

found that the leak of Nord Stream 1 and 2 was likely not an accident. [456]

It was later reported by Danish authorities that there were leaks in two locations of Nord Stream 1. Nord Stream AG, the agency in charge of the Nord Stream pipelines, reported,

"The destruction of three strings of the offshore gas pipelines of the Nord Stream system is unprecedented."[457]

Russian halted all pumping of gas through Nord Stream 1 due to repairs. Though the pumping of gas to Germany was haulted do to Sanctions and Maintenance, there was still gas in the pipelines when it exploded. The Danish energy agency reported that people should stay far away from the Nord Stream gas leak as it is "life-threatening." Germany suspected the damage could only be caused by sabotage. [458]

[456] DW (27 September 2022) Denmark, Sweden view Nord Stream leaks as 'sabotage' https://www.dw.com/en/denmark-sweden-view-nord-stream-pipeline-leaks-as-deliberate-actions/a-63251217

[457] CBC, AP (27 September 2022) Denmark says damage to Nord Stream pipeline in Baltic Sea was 'deliberate' https://www.cbc.ca/news/world/nord-stream-pipeline-damage-1.6597069

[458] Arne Delfs, Elena Mazneva, Anna Shiryaevskaya (26 September 2022) Germany Suspects Sabotage Hit Russia's Nord Stream Pipelines https://www.bloomberg.com/news/articles/2022-09-27/nord-stream-probing-pressure-drop-at-second-russian-gas-link

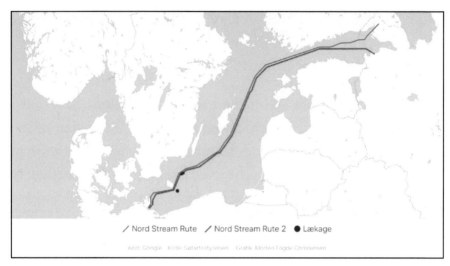

/ Nord Stream Rute / Nord Stream Rute 2 ● Lækage

Kort: Google Kilde: Søfartsstyrelsen Grafik: Morten Fogde Christensen

Figure 61: Map showing where the pipeline explosions occurred—Courtesy DR

The above shows an illustration of where the leaks and suspected sabotage occurred. As a result, the Danish Energy Agency elevated the energy sector to Orange alert, the second highest level possible. The leaks were seven kilometers apart between Karlskrona, Sweden, and the Danish Island of Bornholm. The environmental damage was unimaginable, and the leak, it was said, would last at least two days. It was surprising to see environmental watchdogs and Climate Change activists not condemning the action at all despite the enormous environmental damage to the ocean and to sea life.

In a completely separate event that seems to be a bizarre coincidence, the "Baltic Pipe" was inaugurated the very next day. The opening ceremony was held in Goleniów, Poland. The pipeline will carry ten billion cubic meters of gas from Norway to Poland annually. This pipeline would also enable Poland to transport three billion cubic meters of gas to Denmark, as well as other neighboring countries.

There was mass speculation about who might have been behind the Nord Stream sabotage, but the sophistication of the attack immediately ruled out Ukraine. US naval vessels were in the area a few days before the event, and the US immediately speculated. The White House reported that the Nord Stream sabotage was likely done by Russia, but that argument was very unlikely, not to mention illogical.[459]

Figure 62: President Donald Trump on Fox News with Tucker Carlson—Fox News

On April 12th, 2023, Tucker Carlson interviewed President Donald Trump regarding the Nord Stream attack and asked him who might have committed it. President Trump replied:

---

[459] Paul D. Shinkman (28 September 2022) Russia Shrugs Off Accusations of Nord Stream 'Sabotage' as West Fears Ukraine War Expansion https://www.usnews.com/news/world-report/articles/2022-09-28/russia-shrugs-off-accusations-of-nord-stream-sabotage-as-west-fears-ukraine-war-expansion

"I don't want to get our country in trouble, so I won't answer it. But, uh, I can tell you who it wasn't was Russia. How about when they blamed Russia, You know, they said, 'Russia blew up their own pipeline.' You got a kick out of that one too. It wasn't Russia..." [460]

On February 7th, 2022, Joe Biden, in a news conference with German Chancellor Olaf Scholz, admitted,

"If Russia invades Ukraine, There will be no longer, a Nord Stream 2, We will bring an end to it." [461]

The UK was the second suspected state that could have carried out the attack. UK prime minister Liz Truss was discovered sending a message to US Secretary Blinken saying, "It's done." This occurred one minute after the pipeline blew up and before anybody else knew, according to Kim Dotcom.[462]

---

[460] Fox News (12 April 2023) Tucker asks Trump who blew up the Nord Stream pipeline https://www.youtube.com/watch?v=4ktEFFrtq5I

[461] Lauren Egan (7 February 2022) Biden vows U.S. will 'bring an end' to Nord Stream 2 pipeline if Russia invades Ukraine https://www.nbcnews.com/politics/biden-meet-german-chancellor-russia-ukraine-tesnions-rcna15190

[462] The Washington Standard (2 November 2022) Liz Truss Allegedly Sent Message To Blinken After Nord Stream Sabotage: "It Is Done" https://thewashingtonstandard.com/liz-truss-allegedly-sent-message-to-blinken-after-nord-stream-sabotage-it-is-done/

US Secretary of State, Blinken, reported in a news conference on October 3rd, 2022, that claiming it was a "tremendous opportunity" he stated:

"And ultimately, this is also a tremendous opportunity. It's a tremendous opportunity to once and for all remove the dependence on Russian energy and thus to take away from Vladimir Putin the weaponization of energy as a means of advancing his imperial designs. That's very significant, and that offers tremendous strategic opportunity for the years to come. But meanwhile, we're determined to do everything we possibly can to make sure that the consequences of all of this are not borne by citizens and our countries or, for that matter, around the world."[463]

On February 9th, 2022, Pulitzer Prize-winning reporter Seymour Hersh published a report outlining the painstaking details of how the United States Navy destroyed the Nord Stream pipeline. Hersh outlined how navy divers set explosives on the pipeline and reported how Joe Biden was given the word that it was set to go, but Biden hesitated to give the go-ahead. As

---

[463] Grabien Staff (3 October 2022) SEC. OF STATE BLINKEN ON THE NORD STREAM PIPELINE SABOTAGE: 'THAT OFFERS TREMENDOUS STRATEGIC OPPORTUNITY FOR THE YEARS TO COME' https://news.grabien.com/story-sec-of-state-blinken-on-the-nord-stream-pipeline-sabotage-that-offers

a result, Hersh explained, the delay caused one set of explosives on Nord Stream 2 to become unusable and failed to explode.[464]

The White House denied the accusation, but the mere fact that the US kept quiet on who the saboteur was, immediately implicates the Biden Administration. [465] The German news agency Der Spiegel said they even tried to cover up the guilty party by publishing an article that their investigation implicated a group of six men in a chartered fifteen-meter yacht called the Andromeda. [466] This theory was also quickly dismissed due to the number of explosives used to destroy an underwater pipeline greatly exceeding the cargo capacity of the vessel in question.

Other such incidences of sabotage, include the Russian airbase Engels-2 and the Dyagilevo military airbase near Ryazan, but the clear point here is that Ukraine has been the perpetraitor of all Sabatage events thus far, in this conflict.

---

[464] Seymour Hersh (8 February 2023) How America Took Out The Nord Stream Pipeline https://seymourhersh.substack.com/p/how-america-took-out-the-nord-stream

[465] Anna Skinner (9 February 2023) Nord Stream Attack: Senator Raises Alarms About Alleged U.S. Involvement https://www.newsweek.com/nord-stream-attack-senator-raises-alarms-about-alleged-us-involvement-1780192

[466] Julian Borger (10 March 2023) Divers used chartered yacht to sabotage Nord Stream pipelines – report https://www.theguardian.com/world/2023/mar/10/divers-used-chartered-yacht-to-sabotage-nord-stream-pipelines-report

Sabatage, including the blatant disreagard of environmental factors.

CHAPTER TWELVE

THE WAR THAT COULD HAVE BEEN AVOIDED

A country can rule the world in two different ways: with brute force or with humility. The US can, once again, be the greatest country on earth if we become more humble and respectful to all nations, not just to those we control. The US' conquest of globalism through NATO membership needs to end.

THE INTROSPECTION

I want to conclude this book with my opinion regarding the entire Special military operation thus far. The needless annihilation of almost all Ukrainian cities in the battlefield could have been spared, but due to the efforts of military support from NATO and the EU, destruction is what occurred. I would include the Russian special military operation as well, but I believe the point has been made that this war didn't need to happen at all.

A very popular phrase coming out of NATO and the EU is: "We are not a party to conflict." While proclaiming they are not involved in the war, the efforts made by these countries to fuel the war machine in Ukraine have had insurmountable devastation for cities in the war zones of Ukraine. The devastation to Mariupol, Kherson, Bakhmut, Artyomovsk, and many other beautiful cities in Ukraine are now decimated— apartment homes reduced to a ravaged framework of burning columns and cracked walls.

With all of the devastation to the infrastructure of Ukraine, we must recognize the hundreds of thousands of Ukrainians and mercenaries who lost their lives fighting in an unforgiving meat grinder of war, many with little or no training or support.

Over $150 billion from the US alone contributed to this devastation because of a few warmongers in US Congress and the Biden Administration claiming that Putin would move into the rest of Europe when he is finished with Ukraine—all of this because of a mere "Conspiracy Theory."

The primary goal of the EU and NATO was to keep the war going, and their secondary goal, it seemed, was to one-up the other states to show each other how committed they were to the effort. Millions of dollars were embezzled, and millions more allegedly transferred back to US politicians through a cryptocurrency money laundering scheme—all in the name of protecting Ukraine's borders. History should show that good intentions come with a cost. It's obvious that not funding this war at all would have saved lives and homes and would have certainly forced a surrender a few short weeks after it began.

Hundreds of thousands of Ukrainians could have been talking about the occupation and annexation of Ukraine to Russia, but they won't because those hundreds of thousands of Ukrainians are now dead. Their soldiers are dead because the US gave Kiev the idea that if Russia invaded Ukraine, NATO would be there to help fight the war. But what Kiev considered help was much different than what NATO actually offered.

I can't help but wonder what Ukraine would be like today if the US gave President Putin the security guarantees he requested and moved NATO personnel out of Poland, and other neighboring States, giving Russia a buffer zone against imminent threats to the motherland. Why, with all of the military assets the US has in Europe, would there be a need to creep up further and further to Russia's border?

Russia is a Christian nation and a powerhouse that can't be manipulated, bribed, or corrupted the way other countries have. Perhaps that's the threat our politicians are so afraid of. They can't corrupt Russia. I've read that President Putin can't be corrupted, and people aren't able to find any corruption in him. There is also equal allegations that he poisoned his opponents and manipulated elections.

What I've learned from this war is if you only listen to the media, which gets its information from those who want to conquer the world, you will only know that side of the story. If you do your due diligence and investigate and sift through all of the information available to you, you get a slightly different story, and it is all corroborated by many reputable sources.

I love my country, but our government is broken and corrupted. We are the proverbial ten-year-old bully with a shotgun and continue to endanger the lives of Americans and of citizens around the world. Perhaps if we get a real President in the White House in 2024, things will change, but for now, the war continues, and no doubt, we will continue to finance the destruction of Ukraine—and as one US politician proclaimed:

"...to the last Ukrainian."

R. A. Romero

Table of Figures

INDEX